TOY ARMIES

Toy Armies

Peter Johnson

Photography by Norman Potter

DOUBLEDAY & COMPANY INC.
GARDEN CITY, NEW YORK.

Frederick the Great
was the inspiration of
generations of German
flat tin soldier-makers.
The definitive model
by Hilpert of
Nuremberg was
shamelessly copied by
successors. This is a
version by Aloys Ochel
of Kiel, in the 30mm
scale.

ISBN 0–385–18025–X

LCCN 81–69636

Printed in Great Britain

CONTENTS

The lure of toy soldiers
– in the *Forbes*
Museum of Military
Miniatures in Tangier a
young local visitor
inspects a North
African tableau.

FOREWORD

The most comprehensive collection of toy and model soldiers in the world is housed at the *Forbes* Magazine Museum of Military Miniatures in the Palais Mendoub, Tangier, Morocco. The collection tells the whole story of toy soldiers and is used as the illustrations of this book; how it began is described by Malcolm S. Forbes, Chairman and Editor-in-Chief of *Forbes*, the leading American magazine of business:

This collection actually didn't begin intending to become one.

I was attending an antique auction to bid on very different lots. When a box of worse-for-wear United States First World War Doughboys and another of sailors were offered, back came fond recollections of the hours my four brothers and I spent parading and knocking down each other's toy troops (there's not one poor figure that survived from our youth) and up went my hand.

It's not been often or long lowered since.

As a result, the wing of *Forbes* Magazine's Palais Mendoub, though added to twice, has been overrun and we've had to acquire the nearest neighbouring residence to house the growing forces.

Visitors can look out from the palace of former Tangier governors and see the Rock of Gibralter on the right; on the left the Atlantic Ocean and the scene of the Battle of Trafalgar; directly in front all the ships that pass the Straits pass before unblinking, unsleeping eyes of these toy soldiers.

There are, of course, nattering nanny types who think that if children play with military toys, they'll grow up militarists. Playing with toy soldiers or at being soldiers no more led kids to grow up militaristically-minded than playing with toy fire engines or buses or trucks or bows and arrows created firemen, bus drivers, truck drivers or Indians (of the American versus cowboy variety).

Anne and Peter Johnson located many of these tens of thousands of figures; they created a number of their settings and provided much of the knowledge that we have of what these soldiers represent, who made them, of what, and when. As this book makes clear, the collection offers in panoramic, exciting, visible form a comprehensive history of toy soldiers.

Few among us can fail to renew memories as they look at these pages.

Hopefully, one day readers will enjoy reviewing them 'in person' at their barracks in Morocco.

Malcolm S. Forbes

At the Britains' display
of the 1956 British
Industries Fair, the
Queen Mother's
interest is caught by
her own Royal
Company of Archers, a
recent issue. With her
is Princess Margaret
who, on annual prewar
visits as a child,
assiduously collected
Highland regiments,
box by box.

INTRODUCTION

The story of the *Forbes* Magazine Museum of Military Miniatures, which has formed the inspiration and the illustrative basis of this book, is told in detail in Chapter 33. When Malcolm Forbes originally invited my wife, Anne, and me to visit the Palais Mendoub in Tangier, Morocco, to put his 'wee collection' in order, we little realized that it would take us several enjoyable years and many, many miles travelling not only along the well-trodden highways of toy and model soldier knowledge, but also into the lesser known sidetracks and byways.

In that time we have, with the support of a team of willing helpers, counted, catalogued and cleaned, pictured, packed and posted, dusted, displayed and documented, landscaped, lit and labelled, bid, bargained and budgeted for approximately 70 000 members of the biggest little army in the world – the huge host of miniature soldiers that has brought pleasure to successive generations ever since the pewterers of Europe started using up the excess metal from their kitchen wares to make playthings for their children.

We have met many old friends: the soldiers of Heinrichsen, Heyde and Elastolin of Germany; Lucotte and Mignot of France; Britains, Johillco and Timpo of Britain; dimestore Barclays and Manoils of America. And many new, from a rising generation of model makers, diorama artists, and commercial manufacturers producing 'modern toy soldiers in the old style.'

We have come across uniforms we never knew existed, sets the makers never catalogued, makers who lived and vanished unlisted in the reference books. Because the *Forbes* Collection contains all this and more, it has been chosen as the basis of this story – a story not just about 70 000 pensioned-off troops in Tangier, but the story of toy armies everywhere. For the museum, which is not a private hoard but open to the public every day, covers a scope unheard of among leading collections of military miniatures. It embraces practically every type of commercial toy soldier ever made, many nationalities of maker, and a good cross-section of modern models – connoisseur-built figures and dioramas that could never be classed as children's playthings.

Collectors will find in this book no definitive lists of issues from the various manufacturers, with dates, serial numbers and prices. They may complain that Mr X in Britain or Madame Y in France has been omitted from accounts of twentieth-century model makers. They must look elsewhere – to an extensive bibliography on the subject – if they require long and detailed descriptions of conversion, conservation and collection-display techniques. Above all, this is not a price guide to buying old lead soldiers: auction levels move too fast for any work of record to make claims in that area.

This story has been compiled by talking to people involved in toy soldiers: the collectors, the dealers, the auctioneers, the makers, the designers, the men and women who worked in the factories. It has been buttressed by the published scholarship and expertise of long-established authorities such as John Garratt, and the contemporary contributions of fellow enthusiasts who share their knowledge in publications like the excellent *Old Toy Soldier Newsletter* of the United States. It gains immeasurably, I hope, from the help given by 'soldier men' of the stature of Dennis Britain, who spent 60 years of his life making, selling and loving toy figures. If the Britains section of the book appears disproportionately large, I have no regrets. Britains dominate the collector world, both in terms of following and availability.

Toy soldiers were never made in isolation. They were part of the social, economic, industrial and, often, political structure of the country or continent in which they were produced. What was happening in that country or continent, at that time, influenced how they were made and often was part of the reason why they were made. Therefore I have tried to tell the stories *behind* the armies of metal pouring out of the toy factories in split-pine boxes and shiny red cartons, in monster two-layered presentation sets for the rich boys and as individual halfpenny and nickel figures for the poor. The hope is to interest not only the committed enthusiasts (who know some or most of the stories, anyway), but also the would-be collectors, and, for that matter, anyone who ever enjoyed playing with toy soldiers.

The newcomer will learn, for example, why tin soldiers are not tin nor lead soldiers all lead; how Hitler gave his blessing to wartime production of toy soldiers while the British turned theirs into bullets; why toy Boers in the South African war were given black hats (baddies, of course); why the village idiot is as expensive today as some of the rarest toy soldiers, thanks to King George V; what Princess Margaret collected and why Queen Mary knew the price of things to the nearest halfpenny; how Queen Elizabeth II grew a moustache that put a price on her head; how the greatest maker ever, William Britain Junior, nearly abandoned toy soldiers for a career in aircraft design; who made a set called 'Birth of Jesus Christ, size 2'; how Franco's Moors blasted a toy soldier dynasty into oblivion; why Britains were saved by shrapnel and nearly sunk by Cadbury's Cubs; and how the United States produced the worst businessman who ever hoped to make an honest buck by pouring lead into a mould.

The book relates the background to these stories not only in words but in the pictures of Norman Potter who was responsible for the majority of the photography, *in situ* at the *Forbes* Museum. In taking the pictures of the collection, he and his collaborators have tried to recapture the make-believe and the romance of childhood, without which toy soldiers would be no more than colourful lumps of sculpted lead.

My thanks to those of whom I am indebted in the preparation of this book go first to Malcolm Forbes, who made it all possible. As Anne and I have drilled the Palais Mendoub army into parade ground and battle order, we could not have wished for a more enthusiastic and interested commanding officer. He has filled many roles, not the least those of indefatigable recruiting sergeant, understanding paymaster, generous quartermaster and appreciative reviewing general. My gratitude goes, too, to Robert Gerofi, who has furnished the most splendid barracks any army ever had, and the whole of his staff at the Palais Mendoub who have laboured long with us in landscaping the displays. At *Forbes* in New York, Robert Forbes, who co-operated in some of the photography, Christopher Forbes, Margaret Kelly and Mary Ann Danner have given immeasurable help and support.

A special acknowledgement is due to Dennis Britain, retired chairman of Britains, who has kindly provided much first-hand material about the greatest toy soldier company in the world. The present managing director, Roy Selwyn-Smith, has made available much valuable documentation and photographic material of a historical nature from the firm's files.

From a large circle of collectors, five who are close personal friends have provided much information and sustained my interest in toy and model soldiers over many years. They are: Burtt Ehrlich, Remigio Gennari, Edward Ruby, and Rachel and Milt Sieroty. My thanks go also to members of the staff of Phillips, the international fine art auctioneers who specialize in soldier auctions: David Borthwick, Celia Charlton, Chris Halton (photographer), Charles Russell (photo-librarian) in London, and Tara Ana Finley in New York; their assistance has been unstinting in providing access to records and photographic background material. I enjoyed and gained much from talking to Douglas Fairbanks Junior about his collection, and acknowledge the help of Dr Schmidt of the Wehrgeschichtliches Museum at Schloss Rastatt, West Germany, and Dr Ernst Aichner, curator of the Bayerisches Armeemuseum at Ingolstadt, West Germany. And a special word of thanks to my agent, John Pawsey, for his customarily diligent brain- and legwork.

At a crucial stage in the writing of the book I approached Jo and Steve Sommers, of Oak Park, Illinois, editors of the *Old Toy Soldier Newsletter*, a periodical which I have found makes an immense contribution to the lore of toy and model soldiers because it is written by the men and women who collect them. The Sommers not only gave immediate permission to quote from chosen extracts published in the magazine, but allowed me in their columns to appeal for first-hand information from fellow collectors across the United States, Canada and in Europe, wherever subscribers live.

The latter appeal was still bringing results when the book was going to press. I am particularly indebted to Stacy Holmes who responded with background material including unpublished correspondence with the late Richard Courtenay; and Paul A. Lyon who supplied a fascinating insight into the notably *un*successful business of Moulded Miniatures of Chicago, and contemporary newspaper clippings about toy soldier collections dating from the thirties. David Schacter, another American collector and a friend, wrote to tell of a former Britains employee who used to have a job filling the lead pots in the casting shop before the Second World War; each caster, so went the story, had his own call to summon replenishment and the supply boy recognized the calls – a whistle, a sing-song shout, a bellow – and thus knew from which area of the department they came (Roy Selwyn-Smith of Britains has confirmed the story, pointing out that such a system was necessary in an exceedingly noisy environment).

My acknowledgment and grateful thanks go to many others whose knowledge has been shared with fellow enthusiasts in *Old Toy Soldier Newsletter*, in other publications such as the *Journal of the British Model Soldier Society*, and in personal correspondence and acquaintanceship. They are: Steve Balkin (with whom I have traded toy soldier and other stories whilst cataloguing Stacy Holmes's collection in New York, and later over the bar at the Westbury on Madison), Herbert Bechtold, Will Beierwaltes, Hadleigh St George Bond, Cy Broman, William Carman (an unfailingly accurate and charming source of information), Bill Connolly, Lee Daniels, Bill Driscoll, Cornelius Frazer, John Garratt, Peter Greenhill (who keeps alight the brilliant Courtenay torch), Roger Garfield, G.M. Haley, George Keester, Vic Medcalf (the king of Britains 'civvies'), James Opie, Richard O'Brien (who has taught us all to respect the dimestore soldier), Harold Pestana (whose generosity has hung soldiers on my Christmas tree), Don Pielin, Reggie Polaine (who put composition Germans between hard backs), Stewart Saxe, Jan and Frank Scroby (who delight with Blenheim), Terry Sells, Sonia and Edward Suren (whose Willie figures charm and whose hospitality beguiles), Shamus O.D. Wade, Joe Wallis and Donald A. Wollheim.

There is a huge number of people with whom contact over the past ten years has helped stimulate, foster or fuel my interest in toy soldiers. I include: Steve Ahern, Colin Barber, Lee Barneson, Johnson Bayly, John G. Bell III, Garret Beverwyk, Jim Boulter, Bill Brewer, Richard Buckton, Pierce Carlson, Rudolph Chelminski, William Christensen, Christopher Clemons, George L. Cody, Jock

Couts, Barry and Adam Crossland, Warner Dailey, Frank B. Darcey Junior, Howard Davey, Thomas N. Dawson Junior, Christopher Dobson, J.J. Dolan, Jacques Duchêne, Francis S. Durocher, Robert Emory, C.P. Fearn, Barry Fondiller, Paul Frary, Paul Frechette, Frank G. Frisella, Vance Gerry, Richard G. Gooding, Huib Goudrian, Alain Gougand, J.T. Gunning, J. Duffy Hancock II, Wolfgang Hermann, John Hannington, Roy Hockedy, John C. Holloway, Brian Hornick, Les Humphries, Chester M. Johnson, Trevor Jowett, Dale Karnes, Gerard Kempermann, Ed Kolacki, Richard Lane, Edward Laucus, Charles J. Leonard Junior, Lawrence Levine, James A. Linen, William C. McDade, Bryan Maggs, G.F. Maitland-Warne, Lyle J. Maple, Alan D. Martens, Michael Moorcock, Ken Moorton, Robert Moorhouse, Joao d'Arbues Moreira, Scott Morlan, Susan and I. Andrew Moore, Sabine Mughrabi, Lynn Murray, J.B. Needham, Assad Abdalla Neto, Christopher Newall, G. Ogden Nutting, William Ogden Nutting, Burton Warner Onstine, Terence J. O'Reilly, George Palmer, Paul Paradine, Roy Partridge, George R. Pitt, K.D. Pizey, David Pressland, Roy Pugh, Walter Reinhardt, Robbie Robinson, E. Roche-Kelly, Peter Rudolph von Rohr, David Rowe, Joanne and Ron Ruddell, John Ruddle, Dennis W. Saffro, John Wayne Saffro, Garret Schenck, William R. Schmidt, Dick von Schriltz, Alban P. Shaw III, David G. Sharman, Philip Stearns, Steven G. Stone, Stuart Swezey, Ben Templeton, Wayne Thomas, Louis Tillery, Bob Turner, Peter Turvey, D. Walker Wainwright, Jim Waller, Charlie Watts, Jim Whildin, Alvin Whitehead, Henry I. Willet Junior, Martin Wohl and William F. Wolfe.

Those names are drawn from five continents of the world, and I cannot claim that the list is complete. To anyone who is missing, my apologies, and to him, one, and all, my warmest thanks for talking the common language of toy soldiers.

In conclusion, there is Anne, my co-curator of the *Forbes* Collection, who has shared with me the task of marshalling thousands of soldiers and thousands of words, pored over countless catalogues and attended innumerable auctions, talked and traded toy soldiers from the Portobello market to the Kasbah of Tangier, taken calls at dawn from collectors in California and bid in German at auction in Nuremberg. She started out in toy soldiers, as the *Financial Times* of London once put it – and as she is first to admit, hardly knowing the difference between a hussar and a halberdier, and progressed to cataloguing one of the world's largest collections. This is her book as much as mine.

Photographic acknowledgments

The vast majority of the photographs in this book were taken by Norman Potter. Additional photography was by Robert Forbes (colour pictures 50, 51, 62 and 63), and Enrico Sarsini, by courtesy of SIPA, Paris (colour pictures 75 to 78). In addition, the author's thanks are due to Britains, and Phillips in London and New York who contributed both black and white and colour illustrations.

PART ONE

Continental Power Base

A modern model from the old moulds of Mignot of France is in the solid, 54mm tradition. Mignot concentrated on the glories of French arms, but also contributed soldiers of other nations, if only because its customers demanded enemies to fight in nursery wars.

When Douglas Fairbanks Junior, swashbuckling hero of scores of movie battles, disbanded his private army in 1977, he told me sadly: 'I have no place to keep it these days.' He was despatching to auction a collection of 3 000 lead toy soldiers he had started when he was 12. The first were a birthday present from his equally famous film star father (Douglas Junior was to start his own career in films two years later).

'Later in life I became seriously interested in building the collection, when I found some of my earliest bits and pieces in the attic,' he said. Those 'earliest bits and pieces' were the output of Britains' London factory when the toy soldier firm was gearing up production again after the hiatus of the First World War. 'I can remember that I was so keen, after rediscovering the objects of my boyhood delight, that I contacted manufacturers and commissioned special pieces. A lovely British coronation coach display took me 18 months to make, between filming. Gradually I built up enough ceremonial troops to make up the entire 1936 coronation procession, with some exotic additions such as the camel corps. . . . When I had a home in California I had the collection on display and at times I loaned it out for charity exhibitions. [He was then, in 1977, living in a New York apartment.] But I now no longer have anywhere to keep it on show and that is the main reason for selling it.' Fairbanks at 67 had eight grandchildren. Did he expect any protests from that direction? 'Well, I suppose so, but like me, they have nowhere to display it properly – and how do you split up a collection between eight?'

His pain at parting with his collection must have been to some extent assuaged by the resounding high prices it fetched when it came to auction in London at Phillips, the auctioneers who specialize in lead soldier sales. The prices were arguably helped by the famous Hollywood connection, but they were also achieved at a time when toy soldier prices were experiencing the steep boom of the late seventies. The Fairbanks band of the Royal Marine Light Infantry trebled its estimate and at £800 ($1400 at the prevailing rate) showed an approximate 320 000 per cent appreciation on his investment when he bought it new as a young man in his twenties. 'I am astounded, absolutely delighted,' he said when I phoned him the results of the sale (just over £9000, or $16 000). But the nostalgia was still there as he added: 'They've been in crates for years, but I still know and love every piece.'

Nostalgia is today one of the two greatest spurs to collecting old toy soldiers. The other factor is rarity. The two are related, of course, by the fact that old toy soldiers as we, our fathers, and grandfathers knew them, are no longer made. With the virtual end of lead toy production in the United Kingdom in the mid-sixties – an event which triggered off the collector and investment boom, there came on the scene a number of firms dedicated to the preservation of the species in ranges of 'new old toy soldiers'. But in matters of price and, in some cases, content, there was no way that these new models could be construed as children's playthings. (It must be noted that some of the better-known new makers, falling in line with toy regulations, avoid completely the use of toxic materials, either in alloys or paint.) In toy terms, the lead soldier was dead. In collector terms, he was assured of a future, pensioned off in retirement as a museum piece and – inevitably – as a statistic in investment portfolios.

The rise in value of lead soldiers, which has made them the subject of specialized auctions in many countries in the western world and the target of headlines when sets that once cost a shilling go for many hundreds of pounds, has brought both benefits and disadvantages for long-established collectors. Writing from California recently, a lawyer who has diligently collected the soldiers of

William Britain on a medium scale over the past 15 years, underlined the dilemma: 'The auctions and the publicity about prices have driven a lot of us out of the market. On the other hand, I suppose we should welcome them, because they are making our collections worth more.'

Estimates of the number of collectors vary enormously. A rash of newspaper and magazine articles on the new collector boom have variously put the total in the United States alone at 5000, 10000 and even in excess of 50000. What is irrefutable is that it is a truly international business. When specialized toy and model soldier sales are held in London, as they are frequently these days, Americans, bidding by telephone, telex and telegram, often account for the purchase of half the lots. There are regular bidders from Italy, Germany, Switzerland and France. South American buyers have begun to enter the lists. Similarly, bargain air fares and dollar exchange rates have brought British and other European dealers and collectors over in force when soldier auctions are staged in New York and Los Angeles.

Dennis Britain, the retired chairman of the world's most successful toy soldier firm that bears his name, can justifiably boast that – until the shutdown of lead production – there was hardly a family with boy children in the British Isles that didn't have some of his company's products in the home. Because of a shrewd and aggressive export policy that seldom wavered from the early twenties onwards, the firm of Britains also became a household word in many parts of the United States, in Canada and other parts of the Empire/Commonwealth, and even made inroads into the toughest of markets, Germany, traditional home of the little tin soldier.

This is the subject of the great international toy war that was fought between the makers in the years between the end of the First and the beginning of the Second World Wars, and is dealt with in detail in subsequent chapters. But even in those days, when lead soldiers were principally playthings, there were true collectors, spurred by the imaginative designs and choice offered by the manufacturers, and to whom the bombardment of miniature armies with lethally powerful cannon was sacriligious. Britains, for example, often found itself in the thirties – and even earlier – meeting special orders from collectors for a specific set or sets of soldiers, outside the normal and extensive commercial range. What was to become the British Model Soldier Society was already on the scene by 1935 and there were similarly flourishing organizations in Germany, France and the United States.

In the absence of other documentation, the files of old newspapers sometimes

A colourfully designed box was half the attraction of toy soldiers for children – and still is for collectors, adding a premium to the value of a set. These are early version Britains' lancers, with fixed arm and horse with 'twisted' rear leg.

reveal evidence of collector zeal – albeit often presented as a quirk of human nature on Ripley's 'believe-it-or-not' lines. A clipping from the *Boston Sunday Globe*, provided for this book's research by Paul A. Lyon, collector, of Findlay, Ohio, tells of a collection in the early thirties belonging to 14-year-old John Ogilby, son of a city minister of religion. John's collection numbered 1500 and obviously, judging from the reporter's descriptions, included many soldiers by Britains and the German firm of Heyde, of Dresden. His enthusiasm for toy soldiers was portrayed as something of an oddity, but there was admiration for his approach to the subject by 'cleaning the family car and doing odd handicraft jobs' to pay for his hobby. 'His enthusiasm,' said the paper, 'possibly accounts for a number of boys in the neighbourhood forming collections of their own, but as their enthusiasm reaches a peak and then dwindles, John is hopeful that presently he may secure their armies at a bargain.' As young John Ogilby demonstrated, there is nothing new in toy soldier investment.

From the same source, a clipping of the *Boston Traveller*, dated 28 May 1929, expounded on the 800-strong collection, heavily Napoleonic, of William A. Corby, a professor at the Massachusetts Institute of Technology, and 'one of only a very few collections in the States.' In August 1936, another Boston newspaper, the *Evening Transcript*, was devoting two columns and pictures to the collection of Dr Howard K. Thompson, a prominent local physician, whose hoard included 20 000 extremely rare paper and card soldiers, mainly of French origin. On the rest of the page, torn from that day's issue, the news headlines tell what was happening in the world outside Boston. The Spanish Civil War: 'Brutality of Volunteer Troops in Seville Area'. Local traveller's tales from Europe: 'Boston Woman says England Fears War'. And amid chilling news from Moscow where Stalin was conducting his fearsome purges of officers and officials, conspiracy trial prosecutor Andrei Vishinsky was quoted in a courtroom tirade against the accused: 'The mad dogs must be shot. Every one of them must be killed.'

Toy soldiers have always been a part of world events. The firms which prospered were the firms which kept one eye on the day's news. Throughout its long history from its first, revolutionary hollowcast figure in 1893, Britains made a successful practice of rushing out troops of the opposing sides when war made news, no matter in what remote part of the world. American and Spaniard, Boer and Briton, Japanese and Russian, Italian and Turk, Greek and Turk, Italian and Abyssinian, German and French, British and German – when nations went to war, the protagonists were marshalled, corded into the familiar red shiny boxes ready for the fat Christmas trade.

There was nothing new in such commercial expediency. The deeds of Frederick the Great's conquering Prussian automata had equally inspired the early Nuremberg tin soldier makers of the eighteenth century. Napoleon's trail across Europe left a huge legacy of military miniatures in its wake. Even the world's earliest model soldiers, among them painted wooden warriors found in Egyptian tombs of 2300 BC were perforce in contemporary uniforms to protect the dead owner against contemporary enemies. Politics and events influenced the manufacture and sometimes the disposal of toy soldiers. Louis XIV had battalions of silver toy soldiers, but they were unfortunatemy melted down to raise money for real wars. Many a nineteenth- and twentieth-century manufacturer saw his moulds and metal stocks impounded to make musket balls and bullets in times of national emergency. Britains itself switched production to the manufacture of shrapnel balls in the First World War and parts for land mines and shells in the Second.

In the commercial war between soldier makers chauvinism played a leading part. Lines of demarcation were heavily national. Germany – in the flat, tin products of the Nuremberg and associated makers – dominated the scene for the better part of a century. France, the home of superb, full round, solid soldiers, presented its challenge in the nineteenth century. The United Kingdom, in the wares of the appropriately named William Britain, did not make its mark until it produced the all-conquering hollow-cast in the 1890s. The United States, heavily dependent on foreign imports in the formative twenties and thirties, was slow to enter the toy soldier lists; but paradoxically, collector interest is probably more intense and widespread there than in any other country of the world today.

Patriotic organs of opinion were traditionally heavily on the side of home industry. At the Great Exhibition of 1851 – when the United Kingdom had no toy soldier industry to speak of – the *Illustrated London News* lambasted some German products that were on the market: 'From Saxony comes a large quantity of tin and lead toys of a low class. They are principally intended to represent soldiers, cannon, tables, chairs, cups &c. They bend almost with their own weight, and the colouring matter upon them stains a moist finger, and seriously injures the health if applied to the mouth. They are certainly no better than are often made at school or at home.' Even in 1910 when Britains was comfortably established as not only the strongest toy soldier-making firm in the country, but already successfully challenging the hegemony of Germany and France in that field, its catalogue felt bound to reassure customers that its wares were 'Produced entirely by British Labour' and 'Designed and Modelled by first-class English Artists.' The message was clear: to buy foreign toy soldiers – and particularly German – was unpatriotic, and such messages became extremely strident when hostilities broke out in two world wars.

Bill Brewer, a friend and collector, who runs a small war gaming, stamp and hobby shop in south London, tells a sad story of patriotism gone wrong. When, as a boy, he was evacuated from London to the Welsh countryside shortly after the outbreak of war in 1939, his mother lovingly packed for him his not inconsiderable collection of toy soldiers, most of which happened to be the products of the German firm of Elastolin, which made highly realistic figures in composition materials. On the base of each soldier was the firm's prevailing mark of the late thirties – 'Elastolin Germany'. Lest his new Welsh playmates think little Billy had in any way afforded aid and comfort to the enemy in buying his toy soldiers from Germany, his mother took a sharp knife and assiduously scraped off all identifying marks, thereby depleting any collector value the collection might have in the future. 'I don't suppose it made any difference really,' says Bill philosophically. 'Very few of my stormtroopers survived their years of campaigning as toys.'

Toy soldiers were meant to be played with. And the makers expected them to get broken. How else could such an industry prosper without wars of attrition that constantly called for reinforcements? It is a matter of conjecture how many hundreds of millions of soldiers have vanished for ever. What is even more remarkable, however, is how many have survived – as the seemingly never-ending supply to specialized auctions bears evidence. The story of this, the biggest little army in the world, opens in central Germany in the middle of the eighteenth century.

CHAPTER **2** HILPERT THE GREAT

At the age of 18, Johann Gottfried Hilpert slung a bag containing personal belongings and a set of tinsmith's tools aboard a southbound stagecoach and bade farewell to his hometown of Coburg in central Germany. Ahead of him lay a 60-mile journey to Nuremberg, a hard seven-year apprenticeship amid vats of odiferous molten metal and the clangour of presses and hammers, and a career that was to earn him the remarkable title, 'father of the tin soldier'.

Nuremberg in 1750 was a graceful city rich in historical association and Medieval architecture, but it was also a bustling metropolis on the confluence of important trade routes and a thriving commercial and industrial centre drawing much sustenance from prolific tin mines that stretched south into the Bavarian heartland.

After somewhat sleepy Coburg, where he had spent four years learning a pewterer's basic trade making kitchen utensils with his tinsmith father, Andreas, Johann Gottfried was eager to strike out on his own in the big city. He duly served his apprenticeship, undertaking during that time, like all indentured young men, to keep reasonable hours, go to church and 'refrain from improper behaviour'. At the age of 28 he was accorded the honour of freeman of Nuremberg and accepted as a master tinsmith.

It was by now 1760 and Europe was in its fourth year of war, a truly worldwide conflict that stretched from Canada in the west to India in the east, and one that was to go down in history as the Seven Years' War. At the heart of the dispute the Prussian legions of Frederick the Great clashed mightily, time after time, with the armies of Austria and her German allies. In the end, *Der Alte Fritz* did more than prove the extraordinary potency of his military machine; he forged it as one of the most powerful forces at work in the shaping of a new Europe, bringing Prussia into the forward ranks of the powers and setting his kingdom on the road to aggressive expansion.

Although recurrent warfare had sapped the economy of the central states, it was in this region and time that the German tin soldier, or *Zinnfigur*, was born. Around Nuremberg and neighbouring Furth and at Augsburg, 80 miles to the south, the tin mines were flourishing despite the war, and the tinsmiths they served were seeking new ways to market their wares – and new wares to market. Above all, they saw commercial possibilities in the flat, tin figures they had made as toys for their children from excess metal used in their normal output. The stunning victories of Frederick the Great provided the inspiration. The age of the mass-produced tin soldier was dawning, a revolution that was to make toy armies available to ordinary German children for the first time.

It was led by Johann Gottfried Hilpert, the first commercial manufacturer of tin soldiers to be identified. By 1770 his Nuremberg workshops were well established in the production of a variety of flat figures. At first, his output had had a wholly peaceful and pastoral flavour, with exquisitely engraved and skilfully cast sets representing hunting, farming, wildlife and theatrical subjects. An outstanding series which has survived from about 1780 is a set of 18 castings of monkeys, about 4.5 centimetres in height, bearing their Latin names on their bases. In a world that was fascinated by the discoveries of exploration Hilpert commissioned engravers to copy the wildlife drawings of notable travellers. Some products of his factory stand on their own as works of art. Such a model is his superb master cast of Frederick the Great, a 15-centimetre mounted figure which must have been specially commissioned by a patron around 1777, so fine is its detail. In like manner, as the first maker to produce portrait figures, he set the Prince de Ligne on a rearing charger in 1780, a masterpiece of animation that had its equal in other models of military leaders.

Big brother was joined in his business by Johann Georg, four years his junior, and later by his own son, Johann Wolfgang, born in 1763, the year the Seven Years' War ended. Together, and with the aid of skilled engravers and casters, they developed new ways of mass production and formed a powerful team that dominated the world of toy armies just as Fritz's Potsdamers had dominated the real battlefields of central Europe. The spearhead of their miniature army was a series of 40 types of Frederick's troops – the first of which were the famous

Potsdam Guards – accompanied by French, Russian and Turkish models, usually in a scale varying from five to six centimetres. Packed on a bed of straw in their light, split pine Berchtesgaden boxes, the soldiers of Hilpert went abroad as exports to the United Kingdom, Holland and Russia. Production and income, dwarfing the scope of Andreas's former domestic business in Coburg, grew so fast that the Hilperts were able to put out a lengthy catalogue of their wares. Although soldiers were its main content, the non-military lines were not forgotten: charming rococo garden and festival scenes and a dramatic boar hunt are among some of the firm's finest achievements.

The Hilpert tin soldier dynasty came to an end with the opening of the nineteenth century. Brother Johann Georg died in 1795, son Johann Wolfgang in 1800. The master, Johann Gottfried, lived until February 1801, and the age of 68. He left behind a record that was to inspire a new generation of German designers – and a valuable stock in trade, not the least part of it being his moulds which were bought by a dealer, Johann Ludwig Stahl.

Hilperts are distinguishable by a variety of marks on their bases, among them H, JH, JGH and HILPERT; the figures are often dated. They are recognizable, too, for their distinctive style. John Garratt, the author and collector, puts it succinctly – and with his customarily critical eye – when he observes that Hilpert riders often seem ungainly for their dumpy mounts, that feet tend to merge unhappily into stands, and that faces have characteristically prominent eyes. Despite these aberrations, however, they stand head and shoulders above many contemporary and subsequent makers in terms of artistic quality – and, undeniably, in size, for Hilpert's was the era before the universal acceptance of the 'Nuremberg scale' of 30 millimetres, of which more later.

Certainly under the hand of the next incumbent, Stahl, the figures from the Hilpert moulds showed an alarming decline in quality. Eager to cash in on the family's reputation, Stahl rushed out a catalogue in 1805 listing 'variously finely painted and also ordinary tin figures, and similar works of art available for cash and at the prices stated. . . .' It contained – in the Hilpert tradition – not only military lines, but also 'country scenes comprising estates, pleasure gardens, pasture, sheep folds, hermitage, corn harvest, country dance, village and turkey cocks.'

Stahl's undistinguished contribution to tin soldiery lasted about 17 years and he eventually sold out to Arthur Haring, a tinsmith of Furth whose firm survived into the twentieth century, mainly as a maker of 30-millimetre flats. At some time, Haring disposed of the Hilpert moulds and the family's legacy is today enshrined in a few extremely rare and valuable individual figures and sets – in museums and private collections – and in the influence the firm's pioneering artistry had on subsequent German makers.

CHAPTER **3** SOLDIERS AT A PRICE

While Napoleon's regiments rolled over Europe at the beginning of the nineteenth century another bitter war, based on commercial rivalry, was being waged with miniature figures that often represented the very soldiers that had brought and were continuing to bring death and destructions to the German heartland and neighbouring states. The combatants in this tin soldier war were the firms that had proliferated in the wake of Hilpert's success, in Nuremberg and even more active Furth, in Augsburg, Saxony to the north-west, and farther afield in Wurzburg,

In oval, split-pine boxes with beds of straw, sets of German tin flats often included action tableaux such as this animated group of the Seven Years' War period by a Nuremberg maker.

Hanover, Brunswick and Hildesheim. The victims were inevitably the people who worked to produce the playthings to delight generations of children.

Conditions in the workshops were far from good. There was little or no protection against poisoning from lead, an essential ingredient of the 'tin' soldier. As in Hilpert's day, so throughout the nineteenth century, moulders worked in cramped, ill-lit, low-ceilinged premises which were often medieval in character as, indeed, they were in age. In all fairness, it should be said that the conditions were no better for the master tinsmiths and their engravers, but they had at least the consolation of reasonable rewards for successful efforts.

A 12- or 16-hour day was common. Pay was low. At the Nuremberg workshops of Allgeyer, a family firm which lasted through three generations in Nuremberg, women moulders were employed because they were cheaper than men. They lived on the premises – under terms which amounted to no less than incarceration – and were constantly exposed to harmful lead fumes from the molten metal. As late as 1898 toy soldier factories in Nuremberg and Furth still employed as painters 150 children between the ages of six and 13, a source of cheap labour that did not end until laws were introduced. In the same area, pay was still rock bottom in 1900 when the German toy soldier factories had reached a turnover of one million marks a year. Five hundred women were employed on piece work in the *Zinnfiguren* capital, painting the tin figures at home. To maintain meagre income levels they had to stay up late at night, working by candle or lamp light, with consequent risk to eyesight and general health.

The industry was booming, but the makers, squeezed on one side by avaricious wholesalers and on the other by their own competitors, had to seek every possible source of cheap labour to cleave profits. One family business, begun by Carl Scheller in Kassel (a firm which was instrumental in forming a tinmakers' 'protective' association designed to challenge the dominance of the wholesalers) resorted to possibly the cheapest source of all – convict labour. Scheller's painting and some casting was carried out by prisoners in the fortress jail of Ziegenhain under a remarkable contract that lasted from about 1840 to the end of the First World War. At last, apparently, labour made its protest and during the 1918 revolution that rocked war-weakened Germany the convicts hurled toy soldier moulds from their cell windows into the fortress's moat – from which some were eventually retrieved.

It is quite possible that the moulds were the very same ones used by prisoners two and three generations earlier, for longevity is one of the prime qualities of a good mould of Thuringian slate, the material commonly used by the German tinsmiths. To prepare the slate for tin soldier production, the craftsman would take two small blocks, one surface of each being finely polished so that the two parts fit snugly together when clamped for the reception of the molten metal. On one face, the engraver made the impression representing his soldier figure, then took great pains to engrave a complementary image on the second block, a task which had to be performed with the most minute accuracy.

When the blocks were clamped together a conical opening in the top gave access to a channel down which the alloy was poured to reach the engraved working area of the mould's interior. After almost instantaneous solidification, the mould was opened and the excess metal, or 'flash', was cleaned off the figure.

The earliest attempts at tin soldier making – often a case of a tinsmith using up spare 'flash' from domestic production as a means of providing his children with toys – employed pure, or almost pure, tin. But tin is expensive. And furthermore, in its pure form it is too brittle to stand the knocks of nursery warfare. A silvery white metal, in sheet form it gives off its characteristic 'cry', a creaking noise, when bent. This is caused by its constituent crystals rubbing against one another. To combat the brittleness, and turn out a more economically competitive product, the manufacturers of flats added lead, commonly in a ratio of 40 lead to 60 tin. Other agents, such as bismuth and antimony were included to control the uneven setting times of the main ingredients (lead cools more quickly than tin). Bismuth was additionally useful as a remedy against 'tin pest', the disease which causes tin to degenerate into grey powder if stored long in humid and cold conditions.

The next step in the commercial life of the tin soldier was painting. Many bypassed this stage, being retailed unpainted. Others were sold partly painted: a cavalryman, for instance, would have his flesh, uniform and equipment painted, but his horse would be left in its silvery tin state. A late eighteenth century writer, E.T.A. Hoffmann, told how a little boy found tin soldiers among his Christmas presents and 'proceeded to muster his new squadron of hussars, who were gorgeously equipped in red and gold, with silver swords, and rode such shining white horses that these also might be believed of pure silver.'

Split pine boxes of varying sizes were used to package the soldiers which were sold by weight, from small platoons to entire battles. Small units went in two and four ounce boxes, larger amounts in eight ounce and 1 lb boxes. One, Adam Schweizer of Diessen-Ammersee, whose main trade was small tin jewellery, announced to the public in 1821 that he was offering 'all sorts of tin soldiers' at 24 kroner to the pound and 'a lb of animals for 48 kroner', all unpainted.

Some makers labelled their boxes by name, with the contents described in handwriting, but much confusion was caused for the collectors of a later day by the nineteenth century wholesalers' practice of concealing makers' identity. Clearly the wholesalers did not want manufacturers to become known as the public might have dealt with them direct, so many labels have only the name of the area of origin. Such bullying tactics by the wholesalers, coupled with their unremitting pressure to force factory prices down, led to bitterness in the industry and sporadic attempts by the makers to combine in protective associations. Behind the make-believe armies that brought delight to millions of children lay the realities of a harsh commercial battleground.

Few collectors have seen a Hilpert outside a museum. In the nineteenth century, however, there was such an explosion of tin soldier production, such a spread of the industry to other German towns and other countries hitherto untouched by it, that these factors have today provided that most essential of conditions for a vigorous collectors' market – availability.

Expansion at first was local, to Furth no more than five miles from Nuremberg. Production of the eight foundries in the new centre was soon rivalling that of the tin soldier's 'home town'. The appeal of the tin soldier was catching on like wildfire, even beyond the frontiers of Germany. He began to be made in Aarau in Switzerland and, among other places, Strasbourg, which had long been a centre for the manufacture of paper sheets of soldiers which were designed to be cut out.

Before the end of the eighteenth century, Europe became enmeshed in Napoleonic wars that were to form the inspiration for countless legions in miniature. Significantly, a very early line manufactured in one of the new tin soldier outposts, Schwerin in north Germany, was the Cossack, popular with so many makers because he symbolized liberation from the yoke of Napoleon.

But while Furth hosted a growing band of soldier makers – such as Johann Gottlob Lorenz, whose business was taken over by Gottlieb Schradin in 1852, and J. Wilhelm Gottschalk whose figures are sometimes found signed by his leading engraver, F. Eggiman – Nuremberg hung tenaciously to its reputation as the capital of the *Zinnfigur* world.

Johann Wolfgang Ammon must have disappointed his father by electing to depart from the family tradition of brewing good German beer and turning to tin. But by his twenties he was a master pewterer in 1794 and beginning to make a reputation in Nuremberg as a successful maker of tin soldiers, notably many of the Napoleonic era as time progressed. The family change from beer vats to melting pots was irrevocable. In Johann's footsteps followed his son Christoph (who obtained his master's title in 1836 with three boxes of circus and railway figures and fighting knights), and grandson Christian (who carried on, producing such top-selling lines as British Household Cavalry, Turks and Austrian lancers, until 1921). The family mark: C AMMON or C A.

The world of the toy armies was a chaotic planet about this time, with some of its denizens striding or riding across the landscape fully 15 centimetres high (alas, most can only be imagined from the discovery of a head fragment here, a boot there), while others barely reached their sword belt in height. Little boys given presents of the split pine boxes to add to their collections found themselves having to match in battle four-centimetre Austrian dragoons with six or seven-centimetre Prussian cuirassiers. The toy wars screamed for standardization.

In Nuremberg city, in the heart of its higgledy-piggledy warren of gabled medieval houses, a young engraver named Ernst Heinrichsen (1806–88) was assimilating his trade at the workshops of Johann Ammon. It was in the 1830s, at a time when a combination of the legend of Napoleon, the onset of the industrial revolution, and the expansion of markets were contributing to a tidal wave of tin soldier production. Heinrichsen was the man destined to bring sense to the scale of toy armies, thus ending the physical overkill of tin giants and allowing children to mix the wares of different makers in realistic manner.

In 1839 he set up his own business and quickly prospered through his unsurpassable talents as draughtsman, engraver and businessman. Attracting good designers such as Karl Alexander von Heideloff, he first made a range of sizes – from five to seven centimetres. For Czar Nicholas he supplied a remarkable set of mounted Russian Guards. For less august clients there were small groups of Napoleonic troops or set battle pieces such as the Leipzig Battle of the Nations in

1815. His breadth of vision set the pattern for the Heinrichsen factory in many decades to come, with the firm's designers ranging the world and its history for subjects of inspiration – from the forests and plains of North America to the jungles of the east, from Hannibal's legions to the trench embattled armies of Europe in the First World War.

He wrote *Kriegspiel*, a book explaining to children how to use flats in war games. But his most important contribution was to introduce the 30-millimetre figure about 1848. It had, for makers and customers, the most attractive quality of cheapness. It was easily packaged. Children liked it because it was of a convenient size to marshall into armies on a table – and they liked it even more when, one after the other, manufacturers all over Germany began to adopt what became known as the Nuremberg scale, making their products interchangeable, one maker's with another's. The Berlin or Hanover scale of 40 millimetre was still retained by some foundries, but these figures were produced in nothing like the vast quantities of the 30 millimetre, measured – for the record – from the base to the top of the head of a hatless, unmounted soldier.

The Heinrichsen dynasty – marking its products E.H. or with the first initial and full surname – continued under Ernst's son, Wilhelm, who took over in 1869. A skilled engraver who drew inspiration from the works of celebrated artists, Wilhelm was followed in 1908 by his son, Ernst Wilhelm, who employed the noted Ludwig Frank among a corps of distinguished engravers. With the name of Heinrichsen surviving until after the Second World War, the legacy is vast and the neat grey or brown cardboard boxes are a familiar part of present day auctions of toy soldiers.

Back to the early nineteenth century, however, and to Furth where a rival to the Heinrichsen empire was emerging just about the time that Papa Ernst was getting into his stride on his own account. Johann Christian Allgeyer had started as a maker of children's tin clocks, then he switched to the more lucrative soldiers. three generations of Allgeyers built up a formidable competitor to Heinrichsen, marking their wares ALLGEYER when once the founder's son, Johann Friedrich, had introduced the family name on the bases of figures around mid-century. Some of the firm's figures exist in a scale over five centimetres, but it saw the wisdom of the rival Heinrichsen's standardization campaign and followed suit with 30-millimetre models. Allgeyer armies vanished from the production field when third

An intricate, finely modelled Corpus Christi procession of tin flats, one of the spectacular non-military productions of Heinrichsen, whose founder, Ernst, instituted the 30mm, or 'Nuremberg', scale and brought standardization to tin-soldier battlefields around 1848. See colour photograph 6 for a close-up in colour.

generation Konrad died in 1896 and the business was liquidated. When still boxed, as many Allgeyer sets are found today, identification is made easier by the firm's labels which appeared in five variations during the factory's near-century of life.

There were many others, of course. Some failed to sign their products. Others – mainly the smaller firms – made a practice of moving from engraver to engraver, thus making it difficult to recognize the source factory of a figure. The Nuremberg firm founded by Christian Schweigger, one of the earliest German makers of full-round figures, had a century of manufacture before it ended in 1886, but its products are rarely found today.

Much more remains of the work of Johann Haffner's factory which flourished in the Furth and Nuremberg areas from the 1830s to the end of the century, turning out millions of flats, semi-flats and full-round figures. Haffner came from Heinrichsen's. He and his son strove to conquer the cheaper end of the market (having considerable success in this area with their exports to Britain) and consequently their figures are uninspired, often stilted, lacking the dynamic animation of a good Heinrichsen or Allgeyer. They are also heavily alloyed with lead. Latterly the firm concentrated on Franco-Prussian battles after the war of 1870.

There is a formal discipline, often bordering on pomposity, about the flats that poured out of the German factories throughout the nineteenth century. It is attributed to the traditions of draughtsmanship that were followed almost slavishly after the industry expanded with such gusto in the 1830s. This was in the middle of Germany's Biedermeier period which produced a decorative style symbolizing the bourgeois taste. The style derives its name from Papa Biedermeier, a fictional character whose aspirations mirrored those of the German middle class between 1820 and 1840, and it found expression in furniture and the decorative arts. As tin soldier engravers copied from contemporary drawings and prints, their creations had the pinch-waisted, barrel-chested look of Biedermeier fashions. From designer to designer, engraver to engraver, mould to mould, figure to figure, the look outlived the century as a unifying factor in the toy industry. New moulds were understandably expensive: indeed, when manufacturers sought to meet the demand for semi-flat soldiers it was often a case of re-engraving old moulds with a deeper impression. Finally, it was a member of the inventive Heinrichsen family – Ernst's grandson, Ernst Wilhelm – who made a breakthrough into the more up-to-date, realistic look of twentieth century flats when he re-engraved most of the moulds after his takeover in 1908.

CHAPTER **5** **A FLAT WORLD**

Otto, a rich fur merchant from Leipzig, spent a large part of his fortune on them. Paul, a slater in Dresden, amused his baby son and built a living with them. Bruno, a plumber in Hamburg, went back to the stone age through them. Eduard, a chemist in Vienna, dispensed them by the thousand and when he died his wife devoted the rest of her life to them. Friedrich, a burgher of Wurtemberg, found a gold mine in them.

The magnificent obsession that bound Otto, Paul, Bruno, Eduard and Friedrich in a common interest was, of course, tin soldiers. Theirs is part of the story of the twentieth-century emergence of the tin flat from a toy into a collector's item. It begins towards the end of the nineteenth century when adult enthusiasts started to meet to play soldiers. They exchanged notes and compared figures, experimented in repainting and took the next logical step of making their own figures. The collector had arrived on the field of the tin soldier.

Activity understandably waned during the First World War when tin soldier production in Germany and elsewhere seriously declined, although a few well-known makers, such as Heinrichsen, managed to keep output going at a substantial level. In the immediate postwar period, although economic factors depressed the toy market (as detailed later in the chapters on German composition figures), the collector got into his stride. A German association of collectors, Clio, was formed in 1924. The following year a company with the worthy name of 'Fabrik fur Kulturhistorische Zinnfiguren und Kulturbilder GmbH Kiel' was founded in that north German port. As its description implies, it purported to make a serious cultural and historical contribution through the medium of tin figures, aiming at collectors, but at the same time not eschewing the bread-and-*würst* market of the toy buying public. Far from it: after being acquired by Aloys Ochel of Kiel it was to become the world's biggest producer of flat tin figures. They came in 30-millimetre size, stamped к (for Kiel and *Kultur*), in cardboard boxes trademarked Kilia and Oki, superior painted models and inferior unpainted, respectively.

The firm was one of several that employed the master engraver Ludwig Frank, who died in 1952 at the age of 82 and whose worktable and tools are in the Zinnfigurenmuseum at Plassenburg, near Kulmbach. Frank was one of an elite band of engravers whose work lifted the flat tin soldier into the realms of art. Another was the redoubtable Sixtus Maior (1875–1936), in whose steps his son followed with equal distinction.

Flats by Ochel from the period prior to the Second World War are most readily available on the collector market today, so huge was the firm's output. When expertly painted they are exquisite creations, fully justifying the argument from enthusiasts of flats that the artistry involved in a good example surpasses anything that can be achieved by the maker of a semi or full-round figure. One of the firm's most celebrated series, Aztecs and Spaniards, is a masterpiece of colour and animation. Aztec warriors seem to leap alive in their brilliantly hued plumage and war trappings. The conquistadores shimmer in their silvery armour, even if some of their accoutrements owe more to neo-Gothic imagery than true sixteenth-century fashion.

The quality of these and modern day flats, produced in many towns and cities in Germany, is in large part due to the pressures by collectors during the between-war years to persuade makers to improve their products. Who were the people whose enthusiasm could unite plumbers and merchants, slaters and tinsmiths, chemists and businessmen in a common interest?

Ernst Wolfram was a turner in Leipzig who made guns and vehicles in the round and suitably sized dwellings. He was early on the scene of collector-makers and his products were eagerly sought by other collectors as accessories to their armies from the start of the century.

Otto Gottstein, the fur merchant who poured his exchequer into miniature soldiery, stands head and shoulders above most as a man who widely influenced good design both in Germany and in the United Kingdom. His hobby dominated his life. Always a collector, he financed the issue of a splendid series of flats, many worked by the prince of engravers, Ludwig Frank. The whole of history from antiquity was his canvas, including such novelties along the way as Henry VIII and his wives, and the dandified generals of Louis XIV. In 1930 he took a tin soldier congress by storm in his native Leipzig by exhibiting some breathtaking dioramas. But time was running out for him in Germany. A Jew, he emigrated to England in the thirties. There, he presented 15 large dioramas to the United Service Institution Museum in Whitehall (they have since been dispersed to other

Finely engraved and painted on both sides, flat figures by Ochel represent an Austrian Banater hussar (*left*) and a comrade from the Szekely 'Green Hussars' regiment in the mid-eighteenth century.

Service establishments) and was instrumental in various design projects which formed a seminal contribution to British model soldier making. When he died in 1951 it must have seemed to Gottstein's large circle of friends that Robert Louis Stevenson's words in his essay on 'Crabbed age and youth' were applicable: '. . . but so soon as I have made enough money, I shall retire and shut myself up among my playthings until the day I die.' Except that Otto Gottstein never shut himself up, but made his playthings available to the world at large.

Bruno the plumber – Bruno Hinsch of Hamburg – started, as a hobby, making First World War tanks in the round, then progressed from the horrors of trench war technology to esoteric subjects such as a stone age hunt of wild horses and a gently nostalgic winter sports scene.

Paul Patzch, the Dresden slater, first made a few vehicles in the round to amuse his young son. Then, from 1908, he began to sell them as toys. By 1924 he had climbed his last roof and tin soldiers were a fulltime occupation.

One of those who found wealth in a 30-millimetre world was Friedrich Carl Neckel (born 1906), a Württemburger businessman who turned his hobby into a livelihood and his home at Wandlingen into a workshop-museum. His firm has been making tin soldiers for half a century with series ranging from antiquity to modern times. Most of his soldiers are marked NS. Fields of action that have inspired him include the Indian Mutiny, German South West Africa in the First World War, the American War of Independence and the American West.

Allied bombers pulverized the lifelong collection of Alfred Retter (born 1906) when they devastated Stuttgart. But Retter started from scratch after the war and as a collector-maker produced some imaginatively designed series, including two that would surely justify the claim to be non-military targets: Snow White and the Seven Dwarfs dressed in High Gothic fashion, and a scene taken from an old German legend, *Die Weiber von Weinsberg*, which tells how the women of a besieged town were allowed to go free with anything they could carry, so they came out with their husbands on their backs.

Aztec and Spanish Conquistador clash in battle, from a large set by Ochel who ranged the world in search of inspiration for subject matter.

The Austrian chemist who took to tin soldiers like a drug was Eduard Scheibert (1882–1930), of Vienna. He founded a workshop where his wife, Hedwig, often did the casting while Eduard acted as designer, packager and marketing manager. Together they produced many historical sets and when he died, the capable Hedwig took over until her death in 1960 – one of the few women entrepreneurs in the toy soldier world.

There were many other collectors who became makers and distributors simply by the acquisition of a workbench and stove, melting pot and metal, moulds and marketing sense: men like Euchar Schmidt who founded a most unlikely Red Indian museum in the town of Radebeul, near Dresden, and Karl Mohr, a dental surgeon, who blunted many a dentist's drill engraving slate moulds for his hobby. A touch of madness? Certainly. For what collectors are without it?

The object of their affections, the steadfast tin soldier, goes on to fight new battles. Erich Kastner, author of *Emil and the Detectives*, spoke for the boy in all of them and us when he observed in his childhood autobiography: 'As soon as the battle was decided I used to lay the dead, wounded and unhurt tin soldiers back in their Nuremberg plywood boxes between the layers of wood shavings, dismantle the proud fortress, and carry the toy world and toy history back into our tiny flat.'

CHAPTER **6** ALLONS, ENFANTS

The flat tin soldier, almost a two-dimensional creation, was essentially German. The hybrid semi-solid figure, a transitional stage towards the full-round solid, also found more allegiance in Germany than it did elsewhere in Europe (the

Close-up of a Mignot Zouave, a fighting man modelled by makers of many nations, including those in the United States whose military history records the actions of Zouave regiments on the Union side in the Civil War.

A rare and spectacular model from the Mignot stable – an eighteenth-century ceremonial coach and horses, with walking escort, the whole being over two feet in length.

United Kingdom was notably cool towards both the flat and semi-solid). It is to France that collectors look, however, for having introduced the first successful commercial examples of the truly three-dimensional solid figure.

The making of the solid figure obviously requires more metal than a flat, therefore it was commercially out of the question to consider using alloys similar to those developed by the Nuremberg pewterers, with their high and expensive content of tin. Such soldiers had been made in the sixteenth and seventeenth centuries in both France and Germany, but they were single figures especially commissioned for wealthy patrons such as the French kings.

For mass manufacture the answer was a mixture of lead and antimony. Enter the lead soldier. A figure containing a comparatively high content of lead had an advantage over the tin soldier in that limbs could be bent into position after casting, a feature much exploited by certain German makers who eventually went in for solids. An obvious disadvantage was the danger of lead poisoning, but it was hardly a burning public issue at the turn of the eighteenth and nineteenth centuries, although the pewterers' guilds of Europe had enforced strict rules about the content of lead in pewter tableware from the Middle Ages. The use of lead made the solid soldier a viable economic proposition. It did not make it cheap. Figure for figure, the tin flat could still be made less expensively than the solid: the overall weight of metal in a flat was a fraction of that used in a larger solid, and the tin soldier industry was tooled and experienced for the job. Commercial solids, therefore, had ahead of them a long and hard campaign to fight in Europe when a Parisian maker named Lucotte produced the first examples about the time, collectors believe, of the French Revolution in 1789.

The history of the firm of Lucotte and its figures is hazy. Records are patchy. In the early part of the nineteenth century, however, the name was taken over by CBG, the initials of a triumvirate of makers, Cuperly, Blondel and Gerbeau. The company's story is beset by reorganizations and amalgamations, but by 1838 the firm was under the mantle of Mignot, the present incumbent and today the oldest toy soldier firm in production. To compound the confusion, Mignot still uses the trademark CBG, though no collector would think of referring to the firm's products as other than Mignot.

Lucottes, being early, are very rare indeed. They generally bear the initials LC with the symbol of the Imperial bee placed between them. But here the jungle thickens for the collector because not all were marked. Similarly, some Mignot figures have the CBG mark, others have the words 'Made in France' added to the initials (or 'France', as on present-day Mignots) and yet others are embossed simply 'Made in France'. Many have no mark at all. Experience and intuition are the collector's best guides through this tangle. More about the differences between Lucotte and Mignot later.

From almost the beginning, the Lucotte-Mignot solids were excellent castings from expensively engraved bronze moulds that produce the best results. Undoubtedly inspired by the victories of Napoleon, the figures had an élan in keeping with the glories of France's feats of arms. Anatomical detail, animation and painting were of the highest quality, and a sound choice of alloys that did not cheat to save pennies has produced a stable and long-living metal, rarely susceptible to lead disease if properly cared for.

The French, being the French, concentrated heavily on their own regiments and leaders. The firm's researchers zealously pursued accuracy in the design of the uniforms of Napoleon and his Marshals; just as much care went in to the livery of a drummer of the Imperial Guard or the sabretache of a *chasseur à cheval*. Similar justice was usually done to the armies of other nations when Mignot deigned to lift its sights above the frontiers of La Belle France, but non-French soldiers received nowhere near the same amount of coverage as the native product. Scottish Highlanders, for example, were accorded somewhat cursory attention and given an unconvincingly slimline bearskin. As my collector friends Rachel and Milt Sieroty, of California, have observed in a study of their favourite field of collecting: 'One gets the feeling that Mignot lost interest in the British after Waterloo and did not research later figures as accurately as French and other Continental armies.' A more cynical observer has remarked that the firm breached its own Gallic armour of chauvinism and modelled foreign armies – which, to be fair, it did in some real measure – only because little French boys demanded enemies for their soldiers to fight.

The year 1815 marked the end of Napoleon's dreams and the armies of France never again changed the maps of Europe as they had done when carrying the banners of the First Empire. By the middle of the century, however, the workshops of Mignot were despatching regiment after regiment of the *Grande Armée* to reconquer Europe with an aggressive export marketing policy. In Germany they frightened the *Zinnfigur* high command and spurred it on to thinking 'solid'. They went where Napoleon's troops had never been – across the Channel to England where, expensively priced, they had moderate success in company with the later German solid figures, until William Britain's cavalry counter-attacked with a secret weapon, the hollow-cast Life Guard. Governments found themselves being petitioned by their countrymen to stem the invasion by protecting the frontiers with trade tariffs. With the memory of Lafayette still warm, the United States looked at and liked the French imports. Abraham Lincoln played with Mignots with his son, Tad.

The new figures brought a three-dimensional realism never before known in toy soldiery and a quality of modelling and finish that has not since been surpassed in the toy field, equalled at its best only by the efforts of present day specialists making *model* soldiers rather than playthings. Indeed, collectors argue that some of the Lucottes could not have been meant as toys, so fine is their quality which must have priced them out of the juvenile market.

Despite the confusion caused by different marks, or lack of them, Mignot figures have certain characteristics that help identification. When tied into their original boxes of rich red, bearing the CBG label and handwritten description, there is no problem. Sets traditionally came as 12 foot (always with flag – very French!) or six mounted, with larger boxed sets of mixed figures. the basic scale is 54 millimetres, though larger and smaller sizes were produced. Mignot foot soldiers have slim waists and narrow faces and both foot and mounted men rest on buff coloured or pale green stands. Heads are plugged in separately, the long-necked look being typical of these and some German solids. Mounted soldiers are removable from their horses and they sit their saddles without the help of the prong and socket found in Germany (and some early Lucottes).

How to distinguish Lucotte from Mignot? Generally, Lucotte are better proportioned and the metal is less brittle than Mignot's. Other differences can be charted:

Lucotte infantry	*Mignot infantry*
Oblong stands (except at halt)	Square stands
Front leg bent	Straight legs
Larger packs and shorter bayonets	

Lucotte mounted figures	*Mignot mounted figures*
Horses have long tails, thinner legs	Short tails
Separate saddle cloths and reins	Walking horse has awkward forward tilt

The international respect for Mignot led inevitably to copying and the term became generic for the description of 54-millimetre solids. However, the firm also produced flats, semi-solids and eventually a cheap range of hollow-cast figures in response to competition from the United Kingdom. Today, with a legacy of 15 000–20 000 of the superb old moulds, including Lucotte, the company markets a large range of 54-millimetre models with emphasis on the glories of the First Empire. Gone, however, are some of the more exotic lines. Students of the unusual particularly mourn the passing of number 22A, *Révolutionnaires*, with aristocrats' heads impaled on spikes and dripping blood. But then, obsoleteness is the spur of collecting.

CHAPTER **7** DEUTSCHLAND ÜBER ALLES

Georg Heyde started his business of making soldiers just after the Franco-Prussian war of 1870 when Bismarck's army had stormed through to Paris, an event which presented Prussia with a momentous victory and the toy industry with a whole new field of inspiration. The business he founded ended abruptly in another war when, the Third Reich in ruins, the factory was obliterated along with the rest of Dresden in the British and American bombing raids of February 1945.

In the intervening 70-odd years he and his acolytes gave toy soldier collectors plenty to enthuse and groan about. The groaners argue that his full-round figures are stilted, clumsy, lifeless, that bodies are too long and legs too squat, that rifle-carrying arms are often disproportionately short, that wild inaccuracies abound; they despair at a confusion of multi-sized figures and complain of inconsistencies and vagueness in cataloguing.

But this polyglot, under-documented army of clumsy, misshapen, oddly sized and wrongly dressed individuals achieved an astounding campaign record and – as the enthusiasts point out – got up to some ingenious activities undreamed of by other, more 'regular' troops.

For this we have to thank the genius of Georg Heyde. Little or no personal detail is known of him as, naturally, any records there were vanished in the Dresden holocaust. Heyde collectors who might have made it their business to seek more information about him did not emerge as a historically conscious group until after that time. What is self evident is that he was a shrewd businessman as well as a technician. The position he won as the leading German manufacturer of full-round solid figures, with an output and a market influence that far outstripped Mignot's, has its roots in the state of the country's toy soldier industry during the late eighteenth and early nineteenth centuries.

In Hilpert's time there had been a sporadic trade, particularly around Nuremberg, in 30- to 35-millimetre full-round figures in solid lead, mounted in small groups on baseboards. But this minor industry was soon knocked out by the cheaper flat tin soldiers, which also more than held their own against attempts to popularize the *halbmassif*, or semi-solid figure of German manufacture, a hybrid creature that might run to a thickness of 10 millimetres compared with the millimetre thickness of a flat. It was this semi-solid figure, however, that became a transitional feature pointing the way to the German full-round figure (France, through Lucotte, made the move without the bridging stage of the semi-solid).

Several makers who were basically *Zinnfigur* adherents produced semi-solids and a few experimented with full-round solids: they included some of the well-known names, Ammon, Allgeyer, Haffner and even Heinrichsen. But the semi-solid is an unsatisfying creature, neither flesh nor fowl, and it is not surprising that it failed to catch on in the potential export markets of France, the United Kingdom and the United States.

The solid, sometimes clumsily modelled, soldiers of Georg Heyde, of Dresden, Germany, were not just parade ground automata: they 'did things'. This German cavalry bivouac scene is typical of the designer's ingenuity which went into millions of figures until Allied air raids obliterated the factory in February 1945.

In the present day, to come across a mass of 30-millimetre semi-solids and, for that matter, full-round soldiers of a similar size, in the bottom of a toy box, an auction purchase, is to meet a dismaying sight. It resembles a tangle of metal shavings or a consignment of chopped-up spaghetti: rifles twisted round necks like lariats, sword scabbards wrapped round waists, riders' legs splayed and saddle-socket prongs bent into disconcerting phallic positions. When patiently straightened out, however, and marshalled into ranks, semi-solids or small solids *en masse* can be surprisingly effective.

The transition to the full-round solid had been made when Georg Heyde came on the scene. His catalogues put the date of founding as 1872, but it is believed he was actually making soldiers a little before then. Like any good businessman he looked first at his competitors, and what he found decided him on a course of action that was the key to his success. It wasn't so much *what* his rivals were serving to the customers that interested him, but *how* they were serving it. He noted that boxed sets of soldiers were sold as so many infantry, or so many cavalry, or a mixture of each. But all the infantry and all the cavalry were doing the same

1 The original engraving on metal has given great scope for colourful painting in these flat, 30mm figures, part of a battle between Aztec warriors and Conquistadores of Spain by Alloys Ochel of Kiel, Germany.

2 British Camel Corps, made in Dresden by Georg Heyde's firm, crest a sand dune in Africa. The two central figures, 65mm in height, are of a set which has an inherent· weight problem: the burden of the camel's body and rider causes the beast's legs to sag and crumple.

3 One of the most attractive sets ever issued
by the British firm of William Britain Junior,
the mountain artillery mule battery. The gun,
when pieced together, fires its metal shells –
or matchsticks – with commendable accuracy;
as a marketing weapon, it never failed to hit
its target.

Right
4 Produced in composition by the German
firm of Elastolin, just prior to the war, this
bandsman of the *Wehrmacht* carries a bell
banner, a superb and rare figure which leads a
large Elastolin contingent in the *Forbes*
Collection.

5 Detail from a boar and stag hunt by an early German flat maker in the Nuremberg area. The hunter has the typical long, slim-waisted look of the Biedermeier period, from about 1820 to 1840, a decorative style which was reflected in tin soldiers almost to the end of the century.

6 Illustrating the fine detail of painting in a Heinrichsen group of tin flats is a Corpus Christi procession. Each side of the figure is painted, each side is different.

7 Movement and dash – an Austrian Hussar and a yellow-garbed Prussian cuirassier illustrate the amount of verve and animation put by Ochel into its standard 30mm toy figures. Cavalry like this, from Frederick the Great's time, has been turned out by the million by the German tin soldier industry.

8 The universal German bell banner, this time leading 30mm bandsmen of the Reichswehr Musikkorps, 1915, by Heinrichsen, a firm which spanned two centuries of tin soldier making.

9 With figures like this, marching across the sands, Mignot of France conquered the soldier markets in the nineteenth century with the first successful, mass-produced solid figures in the round. These mustachioed veterans are Zouaves.

10 Modern Mignots are still produced in Paris in the old tradition and mainly from the old moulds. Standard bearers are (*from left to right*): Amiral de France, Bataillon Popincourt, Grenadiers à Cheval, Bataillon Blancs Manteaux and Royal Artillérie.

11 A Mignot horse-drawn army ambulance takes the field to the background of a desperate rearguard action, a setting that was all too often the case in the Franco-Prussian war of 1870 which inspired this model.

12 Mignot, being French, seldom if ever produced a set of soldiers without a colour bearer. Therefore, even when it made the Paris fire brigade, *les pompiers*, the smartly uniformed firemen were accompanied by a flag bearer – and a bugler.

Right

13 In addition to its 54mm, full-round figures, Mignot made soldiers of smaller size in semi-flat form. They are employed here in a rare presentation set representing the First World War, with three scenic layers of French troops in camp and fighting the Germans.

14 Sunset over the desert, and Arabs by various French makers relax by an oasis. On the horizon is the familiar silhouette of an Arab horseman by Britains.

15 Frenetic activity in a cotton plantation scene is the essence of this superb and rare set by Heyde of Dresden. Heyde often did not specify the supposed country in which its creations were set: this would pass for the Caribbean, the southern states of the United States, or South Africa.

16 British bicyclists and British lancers, a
line-up of attractive (and dismountable)
figures by Heyde.

17 Heyde specialized in seated and standing
bands, in contrast to Britains whose
bandsmen were always on the march. This
band, complete with sheet music and
commodious chairs, is showing early signs of
'lead disease', subsequently treated.

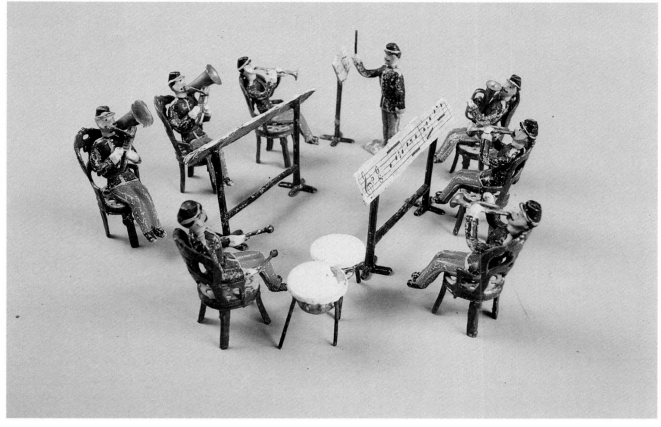

Left

18 Like many toy soldier makers, Heyde
supplied its customers with all the wheeled
paraphernalia of warfare, such as these
pontoon bridging units, kitchen and supply
waggons.

19 The Doughboy goes to war, courtesy of
his former enemy. These American soldiers
were produced for the market in the United
States by Heyde shortly after the First World
War. For picture purposes at the Palais
Mendoub they stand on a sentimental print –
'If I'm not at the roll call, kiss mother
goodbye for me.'

20 Heyde at full spate in a rollicking, action-
filled Western buffalo hunt, howlers and all –
with North American cowboys and Indians
using the bolasses found in South American
pampas.

21 Rare and valuable solid lead characters from Germany, circa 1914, representing characters on the world stage – George V, the Kaiser and his son, 'Little Willie'. They have nodding heads which move disconcertingly when the floor on which they stand is tapped.

22 Denmark's Livgarde, the royal guard, represented by (left) a native manufacturer and (right) by Heyde.

23 'Rule Brittania!'
they sang about the
British Navy. Heyde of
Germany didn't mind
as long as it was good
for business – and
produced this British
admiral and his straw-
hatted bluejackets in
60mm size around
1900.

24 Turk fights Russian
in a desperate
encounter. But a
greater danger looms
for both of them: the
picture shows the
ravages of lead disease,
caused by damp
atmosphere. Prevention
is the best cure.

25 The British Raj at its height in the version by Heyde. This tiger hunt in India, a rare set, has admitted an interloper into the jungle – a tiger from Britains.

26 For pomp and panoply, few sets from Heyde can equal the Triumph of Germanicus, depicting his celebrated return to Rome as a hero and victor. Part of the set (which also includes an elephant) is shown here.

thing. One set would be marching, rifles at the slope, or riding at the trot, another set would be firing, and so on. How much more exciting it would be, he argued, if a child opened his box of soldiers and found them in a variety of postures instead of the one.

It was exactly that excitement that Georg Heyde created. No other maker has produced figures in such a variety of poses. They 'do things'. His troops do more than march, stand guard, shoot and charge. They bivouac with mugs of coffee and bottles of schnapps, climb trees and chop wood, light fires, tend cooking pots, towel themselves, play cards, hang out washing, study maps, uncoil wire, sweep decks, carry shells, feed horses, sleep, fall wounded and lie dead. When they shoot they do so with a metal blob of flame and smoke at the rifle muzzle, a trick Heyde stole from the tin soldier men.

In countless variations of military and non-military activity, from ancient times to modern, Heyde's Dresden factory, latterly at 16 Alaunstrasse, turned out millions of figures that make him a collector's delight. The interest is heightened by his – arguably infuriating – habit of vague cataloguing, so that a set listed baldly as 'Infantry, Cavalry and Artillery' can contain unexpected wonders (incidentally, the person placing the order had to specify the nationality of the figures required). Add to this the knowledge that some sets were catalogued only for short periods or

Heyde was fascinated by the British Empire as a subject, understandably so because the United Kingdom was a good market until the wares of William Britain counter-attacked. British Camel Corps, detachable from their mounts, tread the desert sands of the *Forbes* Museum.

not at all, and hope springs eternal of an uncharted Heyde discovery.

Identification, in the absence of the original box which carried the founder's initials and details of gold medals won at exhibitions, is often difficult because Heyde figures are unmarked as are similar full-round soldiers from Haffner, Heinrichsen and Spenkuch and pirate companies. Heads are plugged in and mounted soldiers have a prong which fits into a saddle socket; their horses are often semi-solid. Heyde infantry steps off on the right foot unlike left-footed Britains. Size is no help at all to the collector seeking guidance because of the bewildering choice offered by Heyde

A glance at any catalogue confirms this. An English-language version from the inter-war years, which uses throughout the splendid term 'fine massive', meaning full round, lists the following available sizes, in millimetres: cavalry – 48, 54, 78, 90, 115, 120, 145; infantry – 43, 52, 58, 68, 75, 87, 120. In addition, second grade cavalry came in 55, 58, 65, and infantry in 40, 48, 55. Adopting the basic scale of an infantryman, the most popular sizes were 43 and 52 millimetre.

Large sets were sold under the headings of 'Battle' and 'Parade', the differences being obvious. They had a varying number of components and were priced accordingly. Parade number 999, for example, is listed as 15 cavalry including band and 31 infantry including band, plus a four-horse team with cannon and limber. International requirements were met quite often by substitute heads and an appropriate colour of paint.

Export-conscious to a degree, Heyde makes use of the vernacular in its English catalogue, liberally sprinkling the pages with the term 'tommies' and in one case, in the description of a traffic set, it talks about 'bobbies'. Elsewhere, the translator appears to have let the firm down with 'Frederic the Grand of Prussia with crutch-stick and 2 greyhounds'. Under 'Aeronaute troops', we are offered '1 balloon mit spring motion'. The potential buyer is warned that if certain army service corps items are ordered singly 'prices suffer a slight elevation'.

The catalogue is rich in special sets, typical of the inventiveness of Heyde. Number 568, an elephant battery has four team animals, a cannon, five mounted artillery men and six palm trees added for interest. The signal corps includes the extra titbit of Morse code instructions to enable you to operate the 'electric flashsignal' correctly. There are Buffalo Bill, Indians and trappers hunting buffalo, a North Pole expedition with fearsome bears and jagged ice floes, even a 'Birth of Jesus Christ, size 2'. And who could resist set 1069, 'Distress landing of aeroplane in Afghan desert', with painted scenery, ten different figures on horseback and 11 on foot?

Take a catalogue of any year and one sees immediately how topical Heyde was. Whenever a war broke out Georg Heyde exploited the market for topicality by rushing out appropriate sets of figures for the Christmas home and export trade, in much the same way that William Britain was to do throughout its history. Sometimes existing figures were adapted to fit the case, at other times new groups were commissioned. Spanish-American, Russo-Japanese, Greco-Turkish wars and the First World War were thus covered, as were campaigns involving the Hereros of South West Africa and German troops, the Boxer rebels of China and many others. British wars in Africa – the Sudan and Boer – received special attention, for the United Kingdom was one of Heyde's strongest markets until the advent of Britains. Indeed, without the United Kingdom and the United States, Heyde would not have been able to develop such a wide range of choice as sales were nowhere near as buoyant as he would have liked in his homeland, staunchly faithful to its *Zinnfiguren*.

In the United States McLoughlin Brothers of New York and the St Louis Soldier Company flagrantly copied Heyde's figures, as did the Japanese. But they had little effect on the sales of the real thing. A collector remembers a visit to Marshall Field's store in Chicago towards the end of the twenties when, as a boy, he found a huge counter in the toy department completely filled with Heydes. 'At Field's I was never able to afford a complete set, but I was able to purchase individual pieces from sets that had been partially damaged in shipment,' he says.

About the same time, a British collector recalls, a minor sensation was caused in Harrods when a sizeable crowd gathered to watch a sales assistant demonstrate Georg Heyde's most ingenious toy. It consisted of 20 redcoated bandsmen with their music stands and a railed podium on which stood the bandmaster. When the clockwork mechanism was wound up the bandmaster waved his baton in time to the tune from a hidden music box. True to Heyde form, the customer was offered a choice of 52 millimetre and 68 millimetre, both playing one tune, and there was also a de-luxe 75-millimetre version with a repertoire of two tunes.

CHAPTER **8** TIGERS AND ELEPHANTS

'By the sacred Ghats of the Ganges, he is truly a monster,' the Maharajah's son whispered to Mainwaring as the slightest rustle of movement in the undergrowth gave warning of the approach of the maneater. Crouched beside his Indian chum in the bamboo 'hide' high among the trees, Mainwaring could hear the thump of his own heart as he nestled his cheek closer to the stock of his favourite high-powered rifle and took aim. The faithful beaters had done their job well. He could hear their cries, their spears beating on tree trunks, their drums throbbing in the jungle beyond the clearing. This was the moment they had all waited for. Soon the deaths of old Baba, his wife, young Ranjit, and the others would be avenged. The moment came sooner than Mainwaring had expected. With one bound, the striped killer broke cover and crouched, snarling with fury, in the open. A flash of orange and scarlet flame exploded from the muzzle of Mainwaring's rifle. . . .

Such was the stuff of adventure for generations of British schoolboys, served in copious amounts by writers of G.A. Henty's ilk and publications such as *Boys' Own Paper*. Now, here it was, British to the core, but in a new, exciting dimension by courtesy of Herr Heyde, a Saxon entrepreneur with a dream factory in Dresden.

His set number 1285, 'Tiger hunting in India', was a masterpiece of marketing. It was assured of a warm reception in Britain, with its red-jacketed, sun-helmeted white hunters, their servants and gorgeously accoutred aristocratic Indian friends. They knelt, firing their explosive blobs of lead, or sat loading, atop bamboo towers reached by bamboo ladders. A goodly number of rungs down the social scale, humble beaters, wielding sticks and spears, padded through a jungle of spiky leaves and palm fronds.

Georg Heyde was shrewd enough to guess that the set would also find popularity in Germany. He knew his countrymen. In the years before the First World War they cast many an envious glance towards the British Empire. In particular, the British Raj in India held a deep fascination. With the loss at Versailles of its overseas colonies, Germany of the 1920s – when the set was still in the catalogue – had no reason to forget its imperialist thoughts. What a temptation it must have been to Heyde to put a version of the white hunters in Prussian blue instead of British scarlet.

Of the tiger hunt sets that remain today, some are missing the leading character, the tiger. He is a fierce looking beast with arched back and bared teeth. He was always corded in as the central feature of the wooden box, prominent among the pieces fixed to a white display card, lying on a bed of straw. One can assume that, once in the nursery, the tiger tended to get segregated with the other animals produced in large quantities to stock miniature zoos – and the marksmen and the armed natives joined the toy armies. In the *Forbes* Collection tiger hunt the

The principal character who, somehow, usually manages to 'escape' from Heyde's set number 1285 representing a tiger hunt in British India. The set, with its white hunters, native beaters, jungle undergrowth and bamboo towers, is in colour in photograph 25.

starring role is unfortunately unfilled and a somewhat tamer, more zoological animal by Britains acts as understudy.

The tiger hunt, representing the high watershed of the British Empire, and another set, recalling the Roman Empire's glory, are two features of the *Forbes* Collection that epitomize the attractions of Heyde. They are chosen for special attention not because they are particularly rare, nor do either of them represent a tableau of warfare. But the tiger hunt and number 1388*, 'Triumphal March of Germanicus', are both typical of Heyde's ingenuity in composing sets of many different poses and activities.

'Germanicus' represents the triumphal return to Rome of the hero. Like the tiger hunt its foot figures are in the 52-millimetre size. In the 60-piece version it consists of a caparisoned war elephant carrying Germanicus, horse-drawn chariots, mounted and foot legionaries, trumpeters, a bear and its handler, wolfhounds and handler (*very* Heyde, these last two) townsfolk, and tall poles flying pennants. It is a highly decorative set, forming a scene that could be augmented to practically any size with Roman figures from Heyde's many series on the subject. The war elephant, for example, was available in another pose – as a charging, trumpeting creature of battle, with armoured howdah and spearmen.

Heyde seems to have had a minor obsession for elephants. Besides the Roman series, they came with Alexander the Great, an elephant hunt with traps, Indian artillery, the elephant battery, and in generous measure in his zoological gardens. For children their appeal was more than the result of an affectionate regard; the elephants provided a very visible component of a parade or a focal point of a battle.

The elephant of Germanicus was one of the prized boyhood possessions of Remigio Gennari, now a Rome architect with one of the largest and most comprehensive collections of Heyde in Europe. He recalls his grief when his elephant, along with his collection, was stolen by the occupying Germans. After the war, Gennari replaced his collection by careful and systematic buying from auctions and dealers all over Europe, and added to it until it reached many thousands of figures – 'Here, there and everywhere, in boxes in cupboards, in corners, and under beds, all over the house,' sighed his wife in the days before he made adequate provision for display. The march of Germanicus was re-constituted. But still the elephant eluded him – until the mid-seventies when I bought one on his behalf in a job lot at a Phillips auction in London. 'It was a great moment when I unwrapped the elephant from his package,' wrote Remigio Gennari. In triumph once more, the elephant of Germanicus had returned to Rome – by express airmail.

*It also came as 1388½ and 1389, the differences probably being explained by slight variations in the number of component pieces.

PART TWO

Britain Conquers

William Britain Junior, whose genius was responsible for the successful commercial development of the hollow-cast lead soldier which took the world's markets by storm. He conjured his world-beater from a vat of molten lead under a cherry tree in his father's garden at Lambton Road, Hornsey Rise, North London.

CHAPTER 9 A MAN CALLED BRITAIN

In August 1980, the magazine of the Smithsonian Institute of the United States, *Smithsonian*, in a major survey of the unique scope of the *Forbes* Museum Collection, referred to the year 1893 and the advent of Britains as 'one of the great seminal dates in toy soldiery'. It was in this year, readers were told, that 'everything in the business turned topsy-turvy when William Britain invented the centrifugal technique of hollow casting.' And with the detachment and clarity of a trained, but lay, observer, Rudolph Chelminski, who had never before written about toy soldiers, went on to describe the process:

Britain poured his molten metal into moulds, as did his competitors, but he added a quick spinning movement to the process, thus forcing the excess lead out through the hole which soldiers possess in the tops of their heads. The result was a perfectly cast soldier, but one which was hollow, lighter and considerably cheaper.

There, in an economy of phrase, was what Britains was all about. How, in a few years, they came to dominate the world of toy soldiers and then held that supremacy for over half a century – to the very end of lead toy soldier making – is a primer course for every collector, and much of the story is a matter of record, well documented and known in chapter and verse by enthusiasts who nevertheless revel in the inevitable mysterious grey areas left by anomalous cataloguing of the firm's gloriously abundant list of issues. Little has been written, however, about the people who made up Britains, undeniably the most remarkable family business in the history of toys. With the help of Dennis Britain, former managing director and chairman, grandson of the founder, and son of William Britain Junior, some of that record can now be placed in its true focus.

William Britain (1826–1906) moved from the Midlands to London at some time before the middle of the nineteenth century. He was a man of entrepreneurial skills and inventive ability and possessed an unshakable faith in the opportunities of free enterprise in Victorian England. His business was the production of mechanical tin toys and the earliest record exists from 1845 when he manufactured at and traded from his suburban home in Lambton Road, Hornsey Rise, North London. In the course of his life and his chosen trade he was blessed with two assets – the name of Britain, a trump card in the chauvinistic Victorian commercial game, and a good-sized, talented and hard-working family of boys and girls who inherited his enthusiasm for ingenious toys.

The toys he produced included walking bears, a Chinese coolie pulling a rickshaw, a man on a penny-farthing bicycle, and a kilted Scotsman who drank a bottle of whisky. Their clockwork mechanism was key or coin operated. A popular steam roller was, the firm believes, the very first British toy to run on a friction drive process still used today. Some of the toy figures were dressed in 'real' clothes and when the Britain family came along, the two daughters played their part by designing, cutting out and sewing the garments. Contrary to popular belief, the production of these mechanical toys did not cease when toy soldiers took over at the end of the century, and some were still being marketed up to the First World War in 1914. Even later they had their successors in productions such as the Britains' fairground roundabout which was an attractive feature of the catalogues in inter-war years; it relied on a child's hand-power and was cleverly promoted thus: 'No mechanism to get out of order'!

But in the eighties and nineties William Britain and his small company were running into trouble. As explained later by one of his sons, Alfred who became the production and business brains behind the firm: 'The mechanical toys were expensive, running up to five guineas. The sale, of course, was limited, and there came a time when we were in a difficult position. Something had to be done, and I had had a sort of hankering after the lead soldier trade for some time.'

The truth was that the lead soldier trade in the United Kingdom at that time was almost 100 per cent foreign. There had been practically no native toy soldier industry, despite a few private incursions into the soldier making field – notably that of a former army captain, William Siborne who produced a massive quantity of tiny (13-millimetre, or half-inch) figures for officially commissioned dioramas of aspects of the Battle of Waterloo, during the first half of the century. In the London stores and those of major provincial cities, Heyde, Mignot, Heinrichsen and Allgeyer ruled in the last decade of the century when the Britains turned their thoughts to toy soldiers. Whether, indeed, it was Alfred, his father, or a combination of family thought that initiated their first experiments is not clear and does not matter. What is known and is important, however, is the role assumed by each member of the family after the dramatic breakthrough.

William Britain's first child was Emily, to whom he left the thriving factory when he died in 1906, a move which led to her brothers buying their sister out and thus providing her with an income for life, while they got on with the business of making lead soldiers. Eldest son was William Junior, born on 14 December 1860; he it was who most earned the title of architect of family fame, the man we now think of when we talk about Britains soldiers. Deft of hand, endlessly inventive, a super enthusiast and optimist, he was, in the words of his son, Dennis, 'a very jolly person, and always on the go, but compared with Alfred, not particularly businesslike'. When he died on 24 November 1933, he had left an unmistakable mark on the playthings of generations of children all over the world and his influence has continued until the present day. William's role in the company was to be, simply, design. He was to become the inventor of the world's first commercially successful hollow-cast toy soldier.

His brothers were, in order, Alfred, Fred, Frank and Edward, and there was another sister, Annie. Alfred, possessing less inventive and artistic talent than his older brother, eventually became the company's managing director under William Junior's chairmanship, and looked after the production direction of the firm. Equally businesslike, Fred was to assume the role of salesman and company secretary. Frank and Edward, the youngest of the boys, eventually took up careers outside the scope of the family business but remained as non-executive members of the board. In the early days, however, all the girls and boys joined in the family enterprise, whose fortunes on one afternoon late in the year 1892 rested in a series of pots of bubbling metal under a cherry tree in the garden of the substantial house in Lambton Road. There, the 32-year-old William was cooking up his invention, the hollow-cast soldier.

He started with a master model, fashioned from a contemporary military print. Through the intermediate stage of a plaster mould, the final brass mould was produced – in two halves, which, when clamped together, offered access through an entry spout. The metal mix was antimonial lead, with a $12\frac{1}{2}$ per cent component of antimony. So far, therefore, the process was no different in principle from the one being used by Heyde in Dresden and Mignot in Paris. Now, however, the wizard of Hornsey Rise was about to demonstrate his unique spell. By pouring the molten metal in through the feet of a soldier and then tipping some out again in a quick, upside-down motion, William found the remainder would set inside the mould like an egg shell. Of course, the metal would not flow out of the mould unless air could get in. That is why every hollow lead soldier has a small hole in the top of the head. In the case of horsemen (who were never detachable from mounts in the Britains' army), the metal was generally poured in the tail and there were small air holes in the horse's nose and man's head. The secret of success was to keep the temperature of the metal just right, and the temperature of the mould was controlled largely by the speed of working.

By the following year, 1893, William was satisfied with the results of his experiments. He, his father, brothers and sisters chose, as the advance guard of what was to be the largest toy army the world has ever known, a model of the Life Guards, the household cavalry of the Queen. It was a mounted figure, fashioned to 54-millimetre scale, with fixed arms and carrying a thin strip of tin as its sword, crude compared with later models, but devastatingly light, lethally economic on metal, and destined to become a world-beater.

Although it later became the practice to fashion the master models in wax – the firm used a high quality French modelling wax to which was added flowers of sulphur for firmness – William's chosen material for the Life Guard was, in fact, plaster which he sculpted with sharp tools. His son, Dennis, has preserved this seminal model – as the company has preserved its stock of brass moulds. These were traditionally cast for Britains by a foundry on contract and because, in Dennis Britain's words 'they were not unduly expensive', new ones were ordered for what were often only minor alterations in detail. Thus when the Guardsman changed from a half-booted to a full-trousered version it was not necessarily a case of chiselling away at the current mould; Dennis Britain thinks it quite likely that new moulds were commissioned.

The Life Guards were cast and trimmed by the brothers. Emily and Annie painted and packed them, five to a set, in the shiny crimson boxes they had made, as they did for many of the early issues. Each soldier was cushioned in a bed of brown wrapping paper in an individual compartment of the box interior. 'I found I could sell five, in a neat box, for a shilling; and they went off faster than we could turn them out,' Alfred reminisced to a reporter nearly two decades later. But it didn't quite happen that way at first. Conservative-minded British stores were suspicious of the new soldiers. Britains' marketing attempts met with blank refusals and the hegemony of Heyde and Mignot appeared unassailable.

Fast-talking Fred was elected salesman by his family and one day in the same year, 1893, he set off by horse omnibus from Hornsey to storm the forbidding bastion of Gamages, an eccentric and rambling bazaar housed behind a gloomy façade in Holborn, London. He carried with him the Life Guards, subsequently marked Number 1 in the Britains' catalogues. Gamages was a shrewd choice. Albert Gamage, a former draper's assistant, who had opened his shop in 1878, could spot success a mile away. He had made a practice of drawing up contracts with small manufacturers to produce lines exclusively for him (although Britains never fell into this comfortable trap). At the store a boy sat on a bench ready to run across London to some cottage industry to collect goods that a customer had asked for. Gamage became a living legend in the London big-store trade. When he died in 1930, he lay in state in the motoring department while members of his staff stood guard like soldiers round a catafalque. They were encouraged to do so by the unprecedented offer of a Saturday afternoon off.

William Britain Senior judged him a likely man with whom to do business – just as he had judged Michael Marks a few years earlier; Marks, the co-founder of the huge Marks and Spencer combine, used to call at Britains' Lambton Road factory with a barrow and collect cheap tin toys – the lowliest end of the family's range – to sell at a profit on his market stall down in the East End.

When, therefore, salesman Fred returned carrying no boxes of soldiers after his foray into Holborn, William Britain, the father, knew that his hunch had been right. Gamages placed a modest order. The new, hollow Life Guards, half the price of some of the Teutonic competitors, were a sell-out. In a very short time Albert Gamage provided an entire department for the sale of the family's wares, which swiftly expanded to numbers 2 and 3 in the catalogue, the Horse Guards and the 5th Dragoon Guards – basically the same master figure regimentally painted by Emily and her younger sister.

The days of walking bears and drunken Scotsmen were numbered in Lambton Road.

Of seven Britain brothers and sisters, Fred was the one who emerged as salesman after his initial breakthrough in persuading Gamages department store in London to take the first sets of Life Guards in 1893. This caricature is from a postcard designed for Britains in 1919 by artist Fred Whisstock, well known to collectors for his graphic box-lid designs.

CHAPTER **10** REVOLUTION IN LAMBTON ROAD

Gamages' success with the new toy soldiers encouraged other stores to stock them; the deal between Britains and the Holborn company was never exclusive, although it enabled the shop to sell some boxes at, say, 10½d when some competitors were charging a shilling for the similar item. Back at the foundry, the Britain family had to make far-reaching domestic arrangements to keep pace with its new-found demand. Much of the rambling Victorian house in Lambton Road was converted into a factory. Whereas William Junior had been the sole caster – as well as designer – additional help was needed and the family took on its first employee, Edward Landen, who became foreman of the casting shop. His daughters have continued to be shareholders down to modern times, an example of the strong family-type loyalty that has been characteristic of the firm.

Fred Britain organized a sound system of distribution through wholesalers. Not for Britains was the pernicious trap of allowing toy soldier wholesalers to put only their own name on the boxes, thus masking the identity of the maker, as had happened in the German *Zinnfigur* industry. In the course of time certain arrangements were licensed to other toy firms whereby two names appeared on a strictly limited number of boxed sets, but for the overwhelming majority of production Britains were Britains, and said so unmistakably in bold printing or cursive lettering on the box label. By the end of the century the firm's boxes were an established part of the birthday and Christmas scene for millions of British boys. Eventually, tiers of shiny, crimson boxes, bearing labels which depicted soldiers in action and listed regimental battle honours, were stacked high in every toy department.

Embossed lettering, bearing evidence of copyright, was to become a feature of the soldiers – on the bases of foot figures and on the bellies of horses, but not before a short, sharp battle with pirates in the early years of this century. In the formative, early years of the 1890s it is doubtful whether the family paid much attention to the risk of piracy, so engrossed was it in its new career.

The size chosen for the new hollow-cast figure was one of 54 millimetre for an infantryman; that is about $2\frac{1}{4}$ inches and represents a 1/32nd scale when related to a six-foot tall human being. It was, Britains found, the most convenient and in time the most popular – although soldiers in 70, 45 and 47 millimetre were also produced in much smaller quantities. The firm never made its figures in the rich variety of postures and actions of, for instance, Heyde of Dresden. Britains' soldiers were essentially for the parade ground or the battle square. Informal poses

Photographed through glass to emphasize their oval bases – a feature of early Britains' issues, bandsmen of the Coldstream Guards parade for the co-curators of the *Forbes* Museum. The set, containing the rare instrumentalist with bombardon encircling his body (*centre, top row*), is avidly sought by collectors.

were rarely produced. The standard foot soldier came in little more than a dozen variations of posture, most of them depending on how he carried his rifle. Variety of regiments and a high degree of accuracy in uniform detail, however, more than made up for this paucity of animation.

While Mignots and Heydes might delight small boys by the way cavalrymen could be unseated, Britains enjoyed no such luxury, being uncompromisingly cast as a unit. There were compensations however, not the least being that ever-popular feature of Britains, the movable arm. The sword arm of a cavalry man could be extended in attacking pose ready for a charge, or could be raised in rallying motion. Similarly, lances could be lowered for business, or carried parade ground fashion. There was, however, little that a small boy could do with rifles carried at the slope on the shoulder, but those held at the trail by running men allowed for realistic variation of movement.

The earliest sets, it must be recorded, were fixed-arm. William Britain's famous Life Guard had a thin strip of tin representing his sword. Movable arms for cavalry did not appear for a few years, when they worked on the principle of a plug which fitted through the body from shoulder to shoulder. Similarly, the first foot models produced were fixed arm with rifles carried at the slope on the right shoulder.

Britains' system of numbering its sets can never wholly be relied upon as a chronological guide. There were many anomalies in the numbering and some-times numbers were left vacant, to be taken up much later by sets which could not possibly have been made in the straight chronological sequence of events. Thus set number 20 would have appeared by 1895 at the latest had it been issued in its correct sequence. Yet this set is a display box of Russian and Japanese infantry and cavalry which we know was issued to take topical advantage of the Russo-Japanese war in 1904. Nearly half a century later the Cossacks were to have a revival because of interest in Russian victories during the Second World War.

In the game of little wars topicality was all. When William Britain made his first hollow-cast, the wealth and might of the British Empire were at their highest. Although major British forces had not been engaged with a Continental power since the Crimean War, there had been some 40 British military expeditions in many parts of the world during Victoria's reign. There was ample material to inspire a toy soldier maker. Memories of the Zulu War in 1879 were still fresh and it was inevitable that several regiments of red-jacketed Tommies would be produced, even if not the 24th of Foot, of Rorke's Drift fame. The Zulus, ever-popular, were issued in the early years of the century, running fearsomely with knobkerries, spears and shields.

The West India Regiment, a colourful unit, their jet black faces marked by staring eyes, was probably ready about 1894 but was held up for the Queen's diamond jubilee in 1897. Other sons of the Empire were also present for the jubilee celebrations – including the first three of many Indian sets, the 3rd Madras Cavalry, the 10th Bengal Lancers and the 1st Bengal Cavalry. They were joined by the Egyptian Camel Corps – freshly and topically reissued again in 1956 at the time of Suez.

Wars did not have to be British or Imperial to inspire the issue of a set of soldiers, as we have seen with the Russo-Japanese. Greece and Turkey in conflict in 1897 produced Turkish cavalry from the Britains' factory; the Spanish-American war a year later was responsible for the appearance of infantry of both sides; much later, but before the First World War, wars involving Italians, Turks, Bulgarians, Serbians, Montenegrins and Greeks all brought forth new issues for the lucrative Christmas trade. Sometimes William Britain looked towards more esoteric fields of warfare for his inspiration, as he did to the Mexican civil wars of 1911–14, a period when the activities of Pancho Villa might have been expected keenly to interest American readers but hardly make many column inches in

LATEST ADDITIONS.

THE VERY LATEST IN TOY SOLDIERS.

No. 188.   Price 2/6

Quite the best method of boxing and displaying Toy Soldiers.

Instead of being sewn on in the ordinary way, the Native Huts, Trees, and Zulu Warriors are securely wired to an artistically designed foreground, with a background attached, shewing hills and trees in the distance, the whole beautifully printed in many colours, and so arranged that the combined effect is most charming and natural.

All the pieces can easily be removed if desired, and the colour scheme used to form other tableaux, both interesting and instructive.

A Certain Seller, but must be seen to be appreciated.

British newspapers. It was from these campaigns, however, that he drew the stalwart figure that was to become set number 186, Mexican infantry, a marching fighter with slung rifle and sombrero. The issue was revived in 1930 for a fresh ten-year life, then vanished, to become today a rare and sought-after item among collectors.

It was inevitable that the Boer War of 1899 to 1902, the most serious and the most controversial for the country since Britains started making their soldiers, should demand several important issues. For the enemy there were only two options: Boer cavalry and infantry. As 'baddies' might be wont to do in those jingoistic days, they came in black hats. Cavalry, as was usual, were five to a box, fixed-arm, four carrying rifles and their leader aiming a revolver. (These Boer riders – who in reality caused much havoc to the infinitely less mobile British columns of regulars – later became the Canadian Mounties, with movable arms, just as a relatively modern issue of a Royal Horse Artillery officer on a rearing horse was, in basic form, the reincarnation of an American Plains Indian warrior.) The Boer infantry at first appeared as a swiftly cobbled job based on the basic British infantryman, with rifles at the slope; in 1906 they were changed to a more warlike figure, standing with bayoneted rifles at the ready, while their officer held sword and pistol. None of the Boers survived the First World War when closer and wider issues made the conflict in southern Africa seem a remote and long-past sideshow.

On the British side, customers of Britains had several sets from which to choose. Of many Scottish regiments involved in the African battles, the firm

London=Made Metal Soldiers.

No 87.   Types of the British Army.
Containing two rows of 13th Hussars.
Price 1/-

No. 86.   Types of the British Army.
Consisting of two rows British Foot Soldiers.
Price 1/-

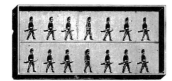

No. 114.   Cameron Highlanders (Active Service).
1/-   Copyright Models.

No. 109.   Dublin Fusiliers.
1/-
No. 110.   Devonshire Regiment.
1/-
(Active Service).   Copyright Models.

Produced
entirely
by
British
Labour.

Only
Innocuous
Paints
and
Colours
and
Spirit
Varnish
used.

No. 112.   Seaforth Highlanders.
1/-   Copyright Models.

No. 113.   The East Yorkshire Regiment.
1/-   Copyright Models.

No. 98.   The King's Royal Rifle Corps.
1/-

No. 97.   The Royal Marine Light Infantry.
1/-
No. 98.   The York and Lancaster Regiment.
1/-

No. 82.   Colours and Pioneers of the Scots Guards.
1/-

Examples of Britains' salesmanship, aimed at both public and trade in a catalogue of around 1910.

issued the Gordon Highlanders, lying, firing. At first, William Britain, it is said, had intended they should be in the universal khaki of active service. But marketing considerations led him to change his mind, and the Gordons appeared – incorrectly, but shrewdly – in white helmets and the full glory of colourful tartans. Britain, it appeared, knew his juvenile market. They were constantly to be best-sellers. When combined with later figures, firing in kneeling and standing positions, they made a magnificent British fighting square. What boy would not prefer to have a square – that symbolic formation of British Imperial steadfastness – in the colourful glories of old, instead of in the modern drab uniforms of the 'new warfare'?

However, it was to khaki that Britain succumbed when he came to design other regiments who distinguished themselves in the Boer War, notably the Dublin Fusiliers and the Devonshire Regiment. In drab uniforms, too, were the City Imperial Volunteers, and the mounted men of the Imperial Yeomanry. These last two issues were to mark turning points in Britains' story. the CIVs were a new, anatomically more sound figure – at the ready – and were the first to carry a date and copyright identification, a paper sticker bearing the date 1900 in their case. They came at the beginning of a period of about a decade and a half in which Britains systematically re-issued many lines, both to improve the quality of anatomy and to keep pace with changes in military equipment. Date stamping was the forerunner of more jealous attempts to defend the company's products from piracy, for now some important copyright actions were pending, in one of which the hard-riding Imperial Yeomanry of the Boer War were to become a test case.

CHAPTER 11 THE PONDERS END FLYING MACHINE

Had it not been for the intervention of fate in the form of a burglar, William Britain Junior might have been remembered today as one of the great aircraft designers, and the history of toy soldiers would have taken a markedly different course. It was, as all acknowledge, William's inventive genius that laid the foundation for Britains' success. Ironically, however, it was that same flair for invention that might have tempted him away from the groundling world of toy soldiers to an entirely different career in the air. The strange and seldom known facts behind this hypothesis encapsule the affair of the Ponders End flying machine.

William Britain was an incurable experimenter – a member of his family remembers him in his later years when, as a chair-bound invalid, he developed an obsession for designing a novel type of castor. It was natural, then, that in the aeronautical pioneering days of pre-1910 he became interested in the challenge and mystery of flight. In short, he designed and personally built a machine which flew, only a few years after the American Wright brothers' historical breakthrough.

After early experiments with models which he flew in the family's large garden, he was encouraged by a Colonel Bowles, who lived on the outskirts of London at Enfield, to consider a real flying machine. From the drawing board that had seen the birth of the Life Guards, the Imperial Yeomanry, the Boer infantry and the rest, came a design for a triplane with two pusher propellors, driven by rope belts from the engine. 'They whirled round like windmills,' says William's son, Dennis, who recalls his own vital part in the building of the aircraft. 'The planes, or wings, were made up of bamboo canes covered with oil silk, which had to be hand sewn. My father had a workshop in which the planes were lain across benches. I was very young and small enough to get underneath the wings as they were sewn. My father would push the needle through from the top, I would take it and push it back up again.' Thus the Britains' flying machine took shape. J.A. Prestwick, a leading name in the field, made a special engine, which was put into place when the machine was assembled at Enfield.

Before it could take to the air, however, it had to be trundled from the residential area of Enfield to a field big enough for take-off. It was moved at the dead of night, not – according to Dennis Britain – to avoid traffic ('two horseless carriages a day'), but to avoid curious crowds in the heyday of pioneer flying machines. At Ponders End, a marshy but flat and open area three miles away, a farmer was persuaded to let a field where a makeshift hangar was built round Britains' flying hope.

And fly it did. 'Not much, to be sure,' says Dennis. 'But it made several hops, about 15 or 20 feet in height. My father was far too crafty to fly it himself. He got a man called Mr Small to pilot it.' A.V. Roe, the British air pioneer and designer, came to Ponders End to view the creation, and William Britain, for a few heady weeks, might have been forgiven for thinking his future lay in the air. But the dream ended one night when an intruder broke into the hangar and stole the aircraft's engine. William Britain was so disheartened that he gave up all aspirations of flight and turned back to his pots of molten lead.

In the early years of this century – and, indeed, presumably to this day – combat men caught by the opposing force wearing its own uniforms and posing as members of that force could expect a summary court martial as a brief preliminary to ending up before the firing squad. Faced with similar masquerades in the toy soldier wars of that time, the high command of William Britain sought a solution in the less drastic, but equally deterrent, justice of the King's Bench division of the High Court in London.

The problem facing Britains was underlined for me personally in the mid-1970s when I was offered a Royal Horse Artillery gun team in review order, its six horses at the gallop pulling a limber and cannon of familiar appearance. The general dealer who had bought the gun team, along with the latest batch of miscellany with which he stocked his niche in the antiques market, clearly had some pretensions to the lore of soldier collectors and assured me that it was an extremely rare and early Britains' production, 'so early that it was before they stamped the name and date on their figures'.

It was not Britains at all, a fact that became clear as soon as a close inspection was made of the gun team, despite the immediate impression given by the galloping horses and the seated men, all of whom had the élan of those early sets from Lambton Road. It was, however an excellent fake – in my opinion, supported later by fellow collectors, a pirate set from the firm of Reka. But in the eccentric world of collecting it was no less valuable for being a fake. The output of Reka, which flourished for about two decades from 1910, was erratic: sometimes good, sometimes awful. Here was one of the firm's better artistic efforts. As it must have been produced a few years *after* Britains' successful High Court actions, one can only assume that Reka's case was that it was not a copy, that a galloping RHA team was, after all, a galloping RHA team, and in this example there were obvious variations from those produced by Britains: for specimen, the cannon's muzzle-sight was very un-Britain, and the way the riders held their whips would have alerted anyone familiar with Britains' toys. Nevertheless, most modern day collectors would regard it as a clever 'steal' and well worth a place in a collection of rare oddities.

Quite early in 1900, when the Boer War was at its height, Britains (as recorded in an earlier chapter) started measures preparatory to dealing with the menace of pirates when the firm placed a proprietory name and date sticker on the underside of the base of the City Imperial Volunteers, then busy distinguishing themselves in South Africa. It was not for a further two years, however, that the company went into court to stop the copying of its designs for 'among other things, metal casts of soldiers and horses'.

In April and May of 1902 Britains obtained the High Court's protection, with costs and damages, against two copyists in respect of the figures of Boer War renown, the Imperial Yeomanry. The defendants were in one case Hanks Brothers

As a result of a series of copyright actions in the early years of this century, Britains felt the need constantly to warn customers against pirates who had been copying its figures. A 1910 catalogue from Lambton Road carried this warning.

NOTICE.

Most of our lines being patented, and others registered and copyright, we wish to caution customers about purchasing inferior imitations of our well-known Goods. None Genuine without our Trade Mark.

Manufactured by

W Britain

in London, England.

and Company, and in the other, James Renvoize. Both these companies, which existed from about 1900 to 1914 as far as toy soldier production was concerned, had flagrantly stolen Britains' design for what was a highly topical and marketable figure. Judgement, handed down by Messrs Justices Wright and Kekewich, was similar in each case, directing that the defendants 'should deliver up to the Plaintiffs all pirated copies or casts together with the mould or moulds or the said Copyright of the said "Imperial Yeoman".' The phraseology varied slightly in one case, ordering the defendant to 'deliver up' or 'destroy' the offending material.

Later that summer and again the following year, Britains sought and gained High Court redress against two other manufacturers, David Mudie and Davies and Company, who had copied the firm's models of the recently enthroned Edward VII. Costs in the case of Mudie came to the princely sum of £50.

The judgement in favour of Britains was based on the Sculpture Copyright Act of 1814. The decision extended to the firm the Act's protection in respect of 'carefully modelled toy soldiers which were anatomically correct and displayed artistic skill and merit on the part of the producer.' Such protection depended 'on the proprietors having caused their names with the date to be put on every sculpture before the same shall be put forth or published.' This ruling produced changes in Britains' system of marking its figures and provided over about the next ten years a codified recognition system of dating that was to be of immeasurable use to collectors of the future.

William Britain was quick to take advantage of the law's decisions by emblazoning them across pages of subsequent catalogues under a large capital letters heading, 'CAUTION'. The announcement carried the magisterial message: 'The Trade generally are hereby warned that Proceedings will be immediately taken against anyone found manufacturing, selling or otherwise disposing of any pirated copies of W. BRITAIN & SONS' Copyright Models of Soldiers, Horses, Statuary, etc. – the 'Statuary' being a fairly obvious reference to Britains' proprietorial lien on the King himself.

In 1911, however, a new Sculpture Copyright Act became law; and it did not cover any of the 1902 and 1903 court decisions on soldier models. What it did was to remove the need for recording the date on figures, a step which many engaged in collector scholarship regard as retrograde. Britains' view was that the 1911 Act had, in many ways, undone much of the good ensuing from the firm's earlier court victories. To this day, toy and model soldier copyright has some very nebulous areas. Where the law is somewhat clearer is in the department of wheeled vehicles, the design of which could be protected by patent.

Copies of the patents of Britains' breech-loading heavy howitzer in 1917 and the boy scouts' trek cart of 1912 (loaned to the author by that most enthusiastic of Britains' fans, Edward Ruby of California) reveal some of the ingenuity that went into the planning of the firm's more specialized toys. The howitzer was revolutionary in toy terms because the design enabled a shell, loaded by breech, to be fired and at the same time leave behind the cartridge, as in the real thing. The scouts' cart could be dissembled into two other types of 'Be Prepared' accessories – a ladder and a camp table.

The gun, both in fixed, siege and tractor-wheeled versions, was made in vast quantities; its popularity rested to some extent on its devastating nursery firepower provided by heavy lead shells which could be propelled from spring cartridges with three, six and nine-foot ranges (an attribute that was lost in post-Second World War years when, in the words of Dennis Britain, 'we were persuaded by the do-gooders to introduce a derisory lightweight plastic shell'). The scout cart was produced in nowhere near as much quantity, having nothing like the howitzer's appeal. With the irony of modern collecting economics, however, the cart is worth twice as much as the gun today.

Britains' early figures – Ancient Britains in the terminology of the game – lend themselves to easy identification thanks to the pirates who brought the legal actions down on their heads. Until 1900, when the firm anticipated the dating requirements, the undersides of foot soldiers' bases and horses' bellies were devoid of any marking. The earliest paper stamp I have seen is the one dated 1 June 1900, placed initially on the new City Imperial Volunteers. With time, of course, these paper stamps tended to become removed, so this ephemeral manner of identification is not entirely reliable. Some embossed naming and dating was to be found on horses from as early as the same year. By 1905, embossing had universally replaced any other form of copyright marking on the foot soldiers, as well as the horsemen.

Dating of new issues was completely abandoned by Britains in 1912, as a result of the Act of the previous year, and the firm retained embossing on both men and horses for the purpose of stating its name, proprietorship and copyright.

For a few years – less than a decade – the firm successfully operated a factory in Paris as an adjunct to its growing export trade. Even before the First World War Britains was exporting to Germany, the heartland of the toy soldier. Oddly enough, exports to the United States were a negligible factor until the early twenties. From this embryo export trade, the markets were to spread across the world – to as many as 50 countries at the peak of the firm's lead production. This tally of countries is even higher today for the firm's output of metal and non-metal figures and diecast toys.

From the Paris factory, in the years leading up to the war when all French operations ceased, came a steady supply of familiar figures, bearing the embossed identification and dating and the word DEPOSE, to show proof of proprietorship. French soldiers, such as the charging Zouaves, dragoons and cuirassiers, were obvious candidates for the Paris market and normally they were produced in sets

The City Imperial Volunteers of the Boer War were the first Britains to carry a dated copyright stamp, initially a glued-on circle of paper beneath the base. The regiment's fame, fostered by news-sketches like this in the *Graphic*, prompted Britains to market the dashing, slouch-hatted figures in an effort to cash in on popular enthusiasm.

MAIN BOER POSITION

ADVANCED BOER POSITION

FRIPP.
JUNE 18 1900
PRETORIA

by Capt Edis . C.I.V)

similar to those emanating from Lambton Road – eight for infantry, five for cavalry. A Parisian innovation, however, was an officer for the Zouaves, who lacked a leader in the home produced version. He was a smart, kepi-wearing figure, walking sedately in comparison with the Zouaves' headlong rush, but he filled an important requirement for the young French public at whom the soldiers were aimed. It was *de rigueur*, William Britain and his salesman brother, Fred, discovered, to provide *officers* in the Gallic market. They must have studied the strategy of Mignot who consistently supplied officer, bugler and/or drummer, and the indispensable colour-bearer in every set of infantry.

Other variations from the French factory (whose production was necessarily ripe for eventual rarity because of its short life) have become keenly sought collectors' pieces. H. St George Bond, a British collector who lives in Geneva, has what must be one of the rarest of the rare French factory products. It is an ambulance waggon, drawn by the usual four-horse team, but it is the uniforms worn by the two team riders that make it unique. These uniforms are the blue tunic, red trousers and red kepi of the French *Infanterie de Ligne*, a version unlisted in any known Britains catalogues. There is no question of repainting or conversion. Bond has had his ambulance team inspected by several knowledgeable collectors who all pronounce it to be genuine.

Britains' French factory had been opened in 1905 in time for a reorganization which, although small in detail, is looked on by collectors as a watershed in the firm's design policy and another important factor in the matter of identification. Up to the year 1906 all Britains' foot models had been given oval or round bases. After that time, these bases were discontinued in favour of square or oblong shapes. With the characteristic inconsistency that makes the study of toy soldier makers fascinating, however, the early shapes were retained for the City Imperial Volunteers, Japanese infantry and the senior medical officers, standing easy in their dress uniforms of dark blue. Why? Who knows? Perhaps William Britain just liked them that way.

CHAPTER **13** INSIDE BRITAINS

'And now,' said Alfred Britain, 'we have practically driven them out of the country altogether. There is scarcely a German-made soldier to be had in the toyshops at the present time.' He was talking to a visitor at the Britains' factory in north London in the summer of 1910, a warm and fruitful season for the firm, judging from the burgeoning catalogue and order books. From Alfred Britain came an enthusiastic exposition of Britains' past and present and a buoyant trade prospect for the future. From the visitor, a reporter called Grubb, has come a rare account of the inside workings of the busiest toy soldier factory in the world.

In the yard a number of pigs of the best white metal had just been delivered. These were transferred, as needed, to the melting furnace where a mass of silvery liquid boiled. One man had the job of keeping filled the little tanks of lead in front of each man in the workshop. Here were no 'sweatshop' conditions of ill-lit, cramped premises as experienced by the *Zinnfiguren* workers of the previous century; in fact, as early as 1895 another reporter* had enthused over the fact that members of the Britain family worked side by side with their employees in airy rooms with 'the sun pouring in at the ample windows and lighting up the faces of the men and boys in the foundry, standing at the casting benches.'

*In the publication, *Athletic Sports, Games and Toys*.

Early days in the casting shop at Britain's factory. The hooded pots in the centre of the bench contained the working stocks of lead alloy, kept molten by heaters. Each caster had a distinctive call, instantly recognized by the boy whose job was to replenish the pots.

In 1910 Mr Grubb recorded in *Boy's Own Paper* that the speed of the foundry process was 'astonishing'. A man held in his left hand the mould, an instrument like a large pair of nutcrackers with the hinged end resting on the table in front of him. The two halves of the mould were fixed about half way up the legs of the nutcracker. With a rapid movement of the right hand the worker drew a ladle of liquid lead from his tank. Almost simultaneously, the left hand closed the mould and a stream of excess lead poured back into the ladle and was promptly returned to the tank. In another moment the worker opened the mould, and with a pair of pliers extracted the lead soldier, all shining silver, and threw it into a basket. Then on to the next one.

The basket went upstairs to a room where a score of girls and women were at work. And here, let's leave it to Mr Grubb:

Each had a small pot of paint before her, and on the table in front were ranged file after file of toy soldiers. Here again the rapidity with which the work of painting the troops is carried out causes the unaccustomed spectator to rub his eyes in bewilderment. A girl has a basket full of Grenadier Guards lying prone and firing, all silvery lead. She takes a pot of black paint and with a deft stroke or two of the camel's-hair brush the 'bearskin' headgear is made to its proper colour. When a sufficient number of bearskins have been painted the same process is repeated with flesh colour for face and hands, and so on until the privates or troopers stand up in the full glory of regimentals.

This was before the days when Britains employed outworker painters – women doing the work in their own homes, a system which was not introduced for another 40 years and then only as the result of a chance happening, as a later chapter will reveal. It was, too, before the days of painting by dipping, a practice to which the firm was to resort for some of its cheaper lines. In this process a basic colour was applied by placing a batch of figures in a wire basket which was lowered into a vat of paint. The painter next operated a handle attached to a spindle which rotated the basket, throwing off the excess paint. The painting was then finished by hand.

In 1910, having observed the painting process, Mr Grubb moved on to another department where the movable arms, cast as separate items, were dealt

51

with. When each had been painted a girl joined the arm socket to the pivot of the shoulder, then passed the figure on to a companion. She, in turn, clipped the arm securely in place with a punching machine.

'My brother, Mr William Britain, always had artistic tastes, and he has designed all our soldiers,' Alfred Britain told his visitor. 'He studies them from life and then models them in wax, just as a sculptor would do if you went to him for a statue of yourself. In fact, he spends his whole time in this way, working out new ideas.'

New that month was a prototype of Britains' lady in 'up-to-date' travelling coat and veil who went with a gentleman in bowler hat and carrying a pipe, to augment the railway station series – a rare and expensive pair today. A bit of an experiment, Alfred Britain had to admit, although he was enthusiastic about their prospects. Enthusiasm was tempered, however, about a recent line which today brings the very top prices among collectors because of rarity: the Salvation Army. General Booth's soldiers and lasses in red and blue had not 'taken on', said Alfred. They did not appeal to the general public, and when it came to soldiers, even the children of Salvationist parents preferred 'the real thing'.

Was it expensive launching a new figure? 'Yes,' said Alfred, taking up the sample of the gowned lady. 'You see that figure . . . well, if you came to me and asked me to make you a piece like that in the first place, I would not do it for fifty pounds. Most of these pieces cost us nearer a hundred pounds to get out. But then the thing's done and we can turn out thousands at little more than the cost of the lead and the labour. The cost of production by our processes is so much less than the Germans' that we can afford to spend more on the initial stage.'

What about the danger from lead? 'None at all. We use no white lead and we are able to show a clean bill to the factory inspectors. The paint is the best in the market, mixed with the best shellac varnish. If a boy holds one of the German toys in a hot hand the paint comes off readily. But our soldiers never shed their colour

The time is the late twenties and farms are booming at Britains. A count of this paint-shop scene from Britains' archives reveals about 30 000 animals awaiting attention from a workforce of about 100 women and girls, following colour charts by hand.

like that, and even if a child were to suck them no harm would happen. So you see, we not only produce a more artistic toy and a cheaper one than our Teuton friends, but also one that is much safer.'

In the yard outside as our reporter left, waggons were rolling up with yet more pigs of lead, ready to be turned into 'a British army corps absolutely correct in the smallest detail of uniform and equipment.' Every week Britains was turning out about 200 000 soldiers, 'ready to take the field at a moment's notice'. And that, recorded Mr Grubb for his wondering schoolboy readership, was equivalent to six tons of lead.

The figures quoted were, of course, surpassed in later years as Britains' fortunes grew. Twenty tons of lead was to become a normal week's consumption and even this amount was increased during times of heavy demand. In the years of peak output, around 1936 and 1937, Dennis Britain observes, it would not have been unusual to see the weekly number of items rise 'to millions, taking into account the farm, zoo and other lines in addition to the soldiers.'

CHAPTER 14 SHRAPNEL-PROOF

Britains, the firm, remembers the First World War as the toughest time in its history. Having closed down the short-lived Paris operation, the brothers feared that the entire factory process in London would have to be terminated because of material shortages and economic conditions. It was, ironically, the very cause of their troubles, the real war, that provided the answer which enabled the purveyors of make-believe war to continue as a business. William Britain's team became part of the war effort.

Someone in the country's department of munitions decided that the lead mix, with $12\frac{1}{2}$ per cent antimony, used in the manufacture of toy soldiers was ideal for shrapnel balls. The firm's casting process was easily adaptable to their production – and was swiftly adapted. The skilled casters who, a few months before, were churning out shining silvery dragoons and lancers – and even models destined to be painted the khaki of hideous trench warfare, turned their hands to the production of millions of shrapnel balls. Among the sidelines there was a contract to produce metal tokens to be spent by soldiers in the officially approved canteens and shops – what Britain has come to know as the NAAFI and the United States as the PX. Together, these government commissions kept the firm going – as, no doubt, similar arrangements helped metal soldier makers in Germany and France.

After the Armistice in 1918, munitions were to provide another bizarre bonus for the company when the government, with vast stocks of lethal material on its hands, sold back to Britains hundreds of tons of shrapnel balls at bargain rates. They became the toy soldiers of the immediate post-war era and Dennis Britain points out: 'We turned our swords literally into ploughshares' – for it was not long before Britains began to produce its farm series, a resounding commercial success that developed out of certain social and moral pressures, as we shall see.

Before the firm turned fully to the war effort, however, it managed on limited resources to produce some soldiers from inferior, thin metal which easily collapsed. Brass, too, was in short supply and finally impossible to come by, so the manufacture of new moulds had to stop and only eight new issues were marketed during the war. In the years leading up to the outbreak of hostilities the juvenile public had been provided with a number of sets representing the nations that were to become Britain's allies, such as the grey-clad Montenegrins at the slope and trail, and the charging infantrymen of 'gallant little Serbia'. By August 1914, and the German invasion of Belgium, that country's troops were also available, as infantry and cavalry in review order.

French *Poilus* marching, in greatcoats and steel helmets, made their appearance. After the war they were described in the catalogues and on their boxes as wearing 'shrapnel proof helmets', an apt if ironic touch considering the fact that it was the re-purchased shrapnel balls which provided the metal from which they were made. A box of French infantry in firing positions, designed and planned for wartime production, had to wait until peace before it could appear. British khaki was to be seen in machine gunners in lying and sitting positions, and steel-helmeted infantry walking with their rifles carried at the trail. Two, more esoteric, wartime introductions were the attractive, skirted Evzones of Greece and the Ghurka Rifles – the Malaun Regiment; both these issues had long catalogue lives which lasted until modern days. Although Prussians, Austro-Hungarians and Turks had been available for some time to provide the enemy in nursery warfare, German infantry in field grey and steel helmets surprisingly did not appear for several years after the war – not until 1931, in fact.

A strange Britains' item which made only the briefest of appearances during the war – thereby underwriting a high rarity value today – was the exploding

The red, shiny Britains boxes became a traditional feature of Christmas in millions of homes. A series of early sets and their packaging is shown here.

54

trench. About a foot long, in cardboard and wood, it was equipped with a target flag which, when hit, triggered a spring mechanism. This caused a violent upheaval of the trench floor which would hurl into the air any troops standing there, simultaneously striking an amorce cap with a frighteningly realistic report. 'The flag should be fired at by one of the 4.7 Naval guns,' instructed the box's label, in a reference to that superb Britains' gun of all work based on the wheeled artillery used to brilliant effect by British naval landing parties in the Boer War. 'Very interesting. No danger!' announced the instructions for operating this alarming trench toy. But there was an inherent danger to Britains' image, believes G.M. Haley, a British collector who possesses one of these rare items. 'Thousands of young men from the British Isles and Empire were going to their deaths at this time . . .,' he has written (*Old Toy Soldier Newsletter*). 'What self-respecting parents would allow their younger children to play with an "exploding trench", no matter how innocently, when at the very same time as those nursery games, elder brothers were perhaps literally getting blown to pieces in the hell that was the war in France?' In the event Britains probably withdrew the trench (Haley's is date-stamped 1915) almost as soon as it was issued. It has never had a catalogue listing.

By the end of the war in 1918 the firm of Britains was reassessing its position and planning for a peacetime future in which its main German competitors were to

be weakened by the economic pressures of the war's aftermath. With an abundant supply of cheap shrapnel balls available for casting, and brass once more made accessible for new moulds, William looked forward to producing new and improved designs with which to exploit the world's wide-open markets. And at Lambton Road his 15-year-old son, Dennis, longed for the day when he could join the firm. Although surrounded by toy soldiers from babyhood, Dennis had always looked on them as 'part of the business'. He had, he explains, never been lavishly endowed with them as playthings – 'It was a bit like the case of the shoemaker's children always being the worst shod.'

He eventually spent 57 years with the firm to his retirement from the chairmanship on Christmas Eve 1978, a record broken only by four years' distinguished and decorated service with the Royal Air Force in the Second World War. At first, however, he had to fight to get a job in the family business. His father felt that his own brothers would think he was unduly favouring his son if he made his path into the firm too easy. Dennis, therefore, began working life as an office boy with the Nestlé Company at Eastcheap in London. He took this business initiation with good grace, if not exactly happily. 'My main job,' he recalls, 'was to brew tea.'

Eventually, at the beginning of 1922, at the age of 19, he persuaded his father to allow him to join Britains on the understanding that he was paid nothing until he had proved his worth. This probation period lasted a year, during which time he settled down to master the craft of modelling and make himself familiar with every part of the factory process. The first to be accepted of many master models he made over the ensuing years was not a soldier at all. It was a horse – a stout, British animal of all work that pulled a tumbrel cart, a line which was to sell in huge quantities and remain in the catalogue to the end of lead production in the sixties. The fertile ground which gave Dennis his first chance was the Britains' 'Home Farm'.

CHAPTER **15** PEACE AND NEW PASTURES

'FROM WAR TO PEACE' was the headline in *The Toy and Fancy Goods Trader* when Britains unveiled its exhibit at the 1923 British Industries Fair in London. The editor confessed it almost appeared that he had exhausted his stock of superlatives when he had reviewed the previous year's display of soldiers. But now here was something 'which from a spectacular point of view eclipsed anything' Britains had ever done. The phrases rolled off his pen like the plaudits of a reviewer at a smash-hit opening night: 'all our expectations fell short of the real thing', 'beautiful', 'comment is unnecessary. . . .'

The event which moved him to such delirium was the trade launch of Britains' toy farm. Previously the exhibit had featured military items, but now the firm surprised its customers by devoting half its display to a landscaped scene representing a village and farm. It was peopled and stocked by the new 'Home Farm' pieces which were to sell in untold millions, a huge variety of lead models that have now become collectors' items in their own right and in forms that still, to this day, pour out of the London factory of Britains in an avalanche of plastic.

The theory has often been put forward that Britains turned to toy farms – and later zoos and circuses – as a result of an anti-militarist decline in the lead soldier trade during the immediate post-war years of the early twenties. There was, undoubtedly, an aversion to things military in those days of change and reassessment; Dennis Britain, who was to play a progressively more important part in the design of non-military lines, talks about the influence of 'do-gooders' who campaigned against war toys. But toy soldier battles went on irrespective of the political and moral climate of the day, and there is evidence to show that any decline in Britains' sales in the twenties – if, indeed, there was one – was attributable to economic factors. What is certain is that the innovative and resourceful family recognized an entirely new mass potential in marketing toy farms, based on the company's production experience of hollow-cast techniques. Significantly, it was in this period that the firm began exporting to the United States and resumed its growing exports to Germany; farms had their place in this export trade alongside the toy soldiers.

Fred Britain, frock-coated and talkative, was present throughout the exhibition and was on hand to explain the company's new 'add-on' farm series to trade and private visitors, who included the King and Queen, George V and Mary. There were, to quote the trade journal, 'cows, sheep, chickens, and every denizen of the farmyard; a lake with ducks and swans, while dotted here and there about the village were to be seen all the familiar figures of country life: a parson, a ploughman, a policeman, the shepherd, and the Weary Willie all found their place in the picture.'

The Weary Willie who caught the editor's eye is not specifically identified – he was probably a farmhand – but the role was soon to be filled unmistakably by Britains' Village Idiot, one of the rarest farm figures. Destined to become a villager with a price on his head of £50 or more for an example in prime condition, the idiot was a lovely model, rustic-hatted and smocked, shod in heavy boots, his cross-eyed face beaming and his chunky body sporting a movable arm which could raise a (metal) straw to his mouth.

Legend has had it that it was Queen Mary who was responsible for the introduction of the idiot, having remarked on the notable absence of this, almost indispensable, character of the English village scene. Dennis Britain has put the record straight. It was, he declares, King George V who, on viewing the Home Farm and village, remarked: 'But where is the village idiot? No English village is complete without him.' Britains remedied the omission with lightning speed and the figure appeared in the catalogues at least up to the Second World War in 1939. Eventually he was dropped, on the grounds of taste Dennis Britain believes, as people questioned the propriety of depicting a mentally deficient person in the form of a plaything.

The idiot's rarity is unchallenged and today he is one of the few farm figures that have become the target of forgers, because of his high value. His price at auction has been passed only by an early version of Britains' curate. He represents a facet of the enormous variety of the firm's farm pieces. Britains thought of everything. It was one of the reasons for the series' devastating success. The firm recognized this in publicity material in its catalogue: 'The Model Home Farm has the additional advantage, that whilst the smallest box of models is a complete toy in itself, any further purchases, whether bought by the piece or in boxes, are fully complementary to previous collections, whether large or small.'

Britains started numbering the farm pieces at 501. These numbers, it should be remembered, never appear on the figure itself, whether it be soldier, cannon, farm or zoo animal, garden item, or even Mickey Mouse, but were the catalogue reference numbers, which also appear on the end-labels of boxes, and in some cases on the box lid itself. The first figure, naturally, was the farmer, with a stick held in his right hand. The arm was movable and this typical Britains' feature, which gave the soldiers so much attraction for generations of small boys, was widely used for a farm population engaged on a multitude of tasks. Farmers' wives followed, one type having an umbrella held in the hand of her movable arm and a basket in the other hand. The first 20 farm numbers ranged through fowls, cocks

BRITAINS LIMITED, LONDON

HIS MAJESTY KING GEORGE V. Reviewing His Armies in Miniature.

With the Compliments of

BRITAINS LIMITED, London, N.

From a postcard issued by the firm – King George V looks in at Britains' display at the British Industries Fair of 1922, as he did every year. He is said to have been responsible for the introduction in the firm's catalogue of the village idiot (*above*), a figure which commands a very high price today because of its rarity.

and hens (white), fowls, cocks and hens (yellow), shire horses, cows, calves, sheep, pigs, 'angry ganders' and other stock.

When the end of lead soldier production in the sixties signalled the advent of universal collector interest, farms were a little slower to take off, but they have now joined the ranks of lead armies in collector esteem. As the series became more popular, a host of accessories poured from Britains' factories: trees and hedges, buildings, carts, ploughs, trucks, gates and fences. Britains' farm buildings are extremely rare owing to the somewhat ephemeral nature of the composition material from which many were made. The tough metal figures stood up to a good deal of nursery wear and tear, but composition cottages were a different matter and few have lasted down the years. Barns and pigsties, rabbit hutches and cowsheds in wood have survived, but in nothing like the same quantity of humans and stock. Britains' large barn and cart shed, with upper floor granary and drop door, would bring an astronomic price at auction today. Similarly, the store shed with corrugated roof (which doubles as an army nissen hut) is a highly desirable piece of farm property despite its humble origins.

There were many other aspects of the Home Farm. The hunt series, one of the designs of Dennis Britain, started life as a farm adjunct with its black and pink clad ladies and gentlemen and hounds. The 'Meet' was a fairly static scene, but the 'Full Cry' gave youngsters horses at the gallop with hounds and fox in similar animation. While this book was in preparation, a collector friend, Edward Ruby of California, raised with the author a query – one of the many Britains' mysteries beloved of collectors – concerning some mounted hunt figures which he possesses. They have on a rear leg of the horses an unusual metal tag bearing the legend, 'Britains England'. It is the sort of tag which can be easily broken off, without damaging the figure. Why and when was this tag introduced? Dennis Britain was able to solve the riddle.

Britains' copyright claim was traditionally stamped on the underbelly of the horse, but these tags were placed on certain figures when the United States import regulations stipulated that goods should bear evidence of the country of origin. This was no problem in a boxed set – the legend could be incorporated on the label, without having to make a special mould by which it could be placed on the horse's belly. With bulk lines meant to be sold individually, however, it was a

Britains always knew how to attract royalty to its British Industries Fair stand. In 1948 the company laid on the full King's Birthday Parade, the Trooping of the Colour, and predictably drew the admiration of George VI and Queen Elizabeth; behind, can be seen Queen Mary, the Queen Mother. Britains did not issue a Trooping set as such, but did have a popular 83-piece Changing of the Guard display box.

different matter. The tag was the answer. Britain thinks this took place in the period immediately after the Second World War, and after a time the regulation grew out of use. Like other production oddities, the tags have added a premium to the value of the figures.

Zoos were another popular line introduced by the firm. The sculptors often visited London Zoo when making a wild animal. As one artist explained: 'We have to get a feeling of movement into the model, and the only way is to see the animal move around.' Many a Britains' elephant has been converted by collectors into a warlike creature, either as an armoured spearhead of an ancient army or as a team animal in colonial artillery. A play for the allegiance of girls was made with the introduction of a metal garden series (still marketed in plastic) and ballerinas. There were many more non-military lines, such as Walt Disney's characters (Dennis Britain designed the successful Snow White and the Seven Dwarfs set, for which he still has the intermediate casts in rough, fusable metal, so vulnerable that 'it would melt in a very hot cup of tea'). Garden gnomes, frogs and newts, toy kitchen pots and pans, a pressing iron, golfers, cricketers and footballers – they all poured from the Britains' factory in a steady stream. But steadfast and profitable, the toy soldier continued to be the firm's main line of attack.

CHAPTER **16** DENNIS BRITAIN REMEMBERS

The overwhelming impression gained from meeting Dennis Britain is that here is a man who thoroughly and wholeheartedly enjoyed his work. From all accounts, the same could have been said of his father. And if this is the mould of toy soldier makers, then Messrs Hilpert, Heinrichsen, Heyde and the rest must have been jolly persons indeed. Dennis, a stocky septuagenarian with a remarkably unlined face, expounds on his subjects with equal enthusiasm when talking about various Britains' products, whether they be his favourite figures of the Zouaves and the Royal Marine band, or the solid model of a frog that inhabits the conservatory at his home in Enfield, north London.

As Britains' written records are regretfully sparse, he is an invaluable source of information on the firm's fortunes from the twenties to the present day. His memories are still vivid and they recall the regular Friday afternoon ritual engaged in by his father and him in 1922. On this, pay day, they would sit at the boardroom table in Lambton Road, filling the wage packets. A good caster – someone who could turn out more than 20 gross, or nearly 3000 foot soldiers a day – would earn about £3 a week. A young trainee girl was on 12s 6d (62½p) a week.

In his initiation into the life of the factory, Dennis gained experience of each department in turn, from the unloading of the lead pigs to despatch and marketing. He soon learned that the bottleneck in production in a prolific toy soldier business was painting. Critical control over the squad of women and girls who did this job had to be maintained so that production schedules could be kept up. It was a happy workforce. Although there was no question of employees addressing executives and directors by their first names, relations were very personal and the Britain family knew its staff and their families well. (When Dennis Britain retired from the chairmanship in 1979 four members of the board, present or recent past, had joined him straight from school.) In the twenties it was, of course, easy to maintain a close relationship with staff when the premises were all under one roof. Even later, however, when the factories proliferated and outworker painters were employed, harmonious and close relations were the keynote of the Britains' work process.

Dennis recalls 'something akin to horror' when, returning from the war in 1946, he discovered that his brother had welcomed a trade union for the first time into the Britains' organization: 'We had seven shop stewards, all girls. I called the entire staff to a talk and explained to them that, as head of the company, my door was always open to anyone who had a problem or a grievance to discuss. Every one of the shop stewards resigned. Now, of course, unions are represented in every department. It's still a happy shop, and we've never had a serious strike.'

Contrary to common repute, Britains did not employ outworkers on painting – a cottage industry of women earning money for spare time work – until comparatively recently in the company's life, after the Second World War, in fact. The system developed then only because one girl, 'the best painter we had, a terrific worker', got married and left. She asked if she could do some work at home

Handpainting of models was always undertaken inside the factory until the development of the outworker system after the Second World War. This photograph from Britains' archives can be dated as some time after 1937 as the employee is putting finishing touches to a State Coach postilion.

and was supplied with a Britains' painting kit. It seemed such a good idea that very soon arrangements had been made to employ 3000 women and girls in similar fashion. Six depots were set up in north and east London and the women collected the work from these centres, returning the finished products there in due course.

For a time, Dennis worked alongside a woman modeller called Wilcox. She was already there when he joined the firm in the early twenties and she stayed at work through about two decades, being responsible, like Dennis, for many of the new issues in a vast production schedule that ranged from girl guides to record breaking speed cars that were capturing headlines on the Utah salt flats. (At an interview session I had with Dennis at his home, his wife reminded him fondly, 'You made a lovely tortoise.')

He also worked closely with Fred Whisstock, the artist whose label creations are well known by and beloved of collectors in these days. A set of soldiers in its original box is worth more than a similar, unboxed set, all other things being equal. If the label on the box is one of those drawn by Whisstock, then a further premium may be added to the collector price. His work ranged from dramatic lettering, designed to appeal to the juvenile customer, to pictorial representations of soldiers in battle or on the parade ground. His style was distinctive, an inherent feature of Britains' between-wars production, and his output was prolific.

Whisstock lived at Southend-on-Sea and there, it is presumed, he had met another resident of the resort, Fred Britain. (Dennis, incidentally, discounts a commonly held theory that set number 37, the band of the Coldstream Guards, out in time for Christmas 1895, was issued because the regimental bandsmen had played on the promenade in Fred Britain's hometown resort during the previous summer). Whisstock was a freelance who accepted artistic commissions from Britains, set by set; he was never so busy as during the firm's gigantic outpourings of the thirties.

Such a range of sets, each involving separate labelling and cataloguing, would have been the despair of modern production and marketing specialists. It was, admits Dennis Britain, 'a nightmare'. People at the top of the firm sometimes feared that the system would break down under continuing and new demands. When, in the thirties, Dennis signed a deal with Cadbury's cocoa to make the Cadbury Cubs – a series of colourfully dressed anthropomorphic animals – to be placed in packets of cocoa to attract children, both the cocoa firm and the Britains factory were utterly unprepared for the result. The gimmick was a sensational success, the demand for Cub-carrying packets being so great that it seemed that the normal production of soldiers, farms and zoos, would be endangered by the new contract.

Britains solved the problem by opening a new factory at Colne in Lancashire. It was in business until the war in 1939, existing solely for the supply of Cadbury Cubs, apart from a digression into whisky, another of Dennis's money-making sidelines. This deal was arranged to aid the exports of Johnnie Walker whisky. Britains supplied millions of small, antimonial lead models of the famous walking figure, which were used as tags with which to tear off the foil cap covering the stopper on export bottles. No present-day collector who professes to cover the field of Britains' non-military 'funnies' considers his collection complete without one of these Scotch whisky talismen.

Against this background of intensive production and marketing diversification, there were yearly highlights to which the family and its employees looked

Dennis Britain, son of William Britain Junior, entered the family firm in 1922 at the age of 19 and retired as chairman 56 years later. He played a leading role in the firm's massive output of the thirties and its development into diecast toys and plastics in postwar years.

forward, such as the London junket of the British Industries Fair and occasional Empire exhibitions, when Britains' armies and its more pacific representatives went on display for trade public and royalty, especially royalty.

Among the exalted, one of the most attentive and critical customers was Queen Mary, consort of King George V. Every year at the Industries Fair she placed an order for Britains' products, usually something from the firm's household utensils range; in a phrase, pots and pans fit for a queen. 'She would become rather upset if the price had gone up, by as little as a halfpenny, from the previous year,' recalls Dennis Britain. 'She knew precisely the price she had paid before.'

On one occasion, there was a minor domestic schism in the York family when the Duchess, later Queen and Queen Mother, sought the attention of her husband, the King-to-be, for a Britains' farm display. 'Bertie! Bertie! Bertie!' she called, with rising impatience. But Bertie was oblivious, lost in the glories of a parade of Britains' new issues of the army's line infantry regiments.

Princess Margaret, not yet ten when the Second World War broke out, bought every set of Scottish soldiers as it was issued. If she still has them, she owns a collection of considerable value. Such selective buying, albeit by royalty, illustrates the fact that 'collecting' is by no means a new phenomenon, born of rarity and obsolescence.

William Carman, who has been responsible for his own range of excellent, solid figures, remembers being part of a small group of collectors who met in the Jacobean Room of the Rendezvous Restaurant in Soho, London, on 15 May 1935, under the auspices of the German refugee Otto Gottstein, 'father' of a new breed of tin flats. The object of the meeting was to form an organization that was to become the British Model Soldier Society. 'If you had Britains,' he has written in the Society's Journal, 'you either made a vast parade or converted them into something new, thus diminishing their value by present standards but at least achieving something "sensational" for those days. The changing of heads even with a matchstick was an event. The cutting of dowelling to make drums was a new milestone. . . .' The meeting itself was a milestone, affording collector recognition to Britains' toys. And there to see justice done, was the firm's representative, Dennis Britain.

CHAPTER **17** GETTING THE PRICE RIGHT

In the autumn of 1977 when Douglas Fairbanks Junior, the film star, sold his collection of Britains' toy soldiers in the London salerooms of Phillips, the fine art auctioneers, a 21-man band of the scarlet-coated Royal Marine Light Infantry – forerunner of the Royal Marines – made headlines in two continents when a Chicago businessman and collector paid £800 for it, then a record price for a set of toy figures. Journalists on both sides of the Atlantic pointed out that Fairbanks must have paid about five shillings (or $1.25, with the dollar at nearly 5 to the £) when he bought the set new in the thirties, a respectable record of appreciation notwithstanding inflation.

Such comparisons have little economic relevance and serve only as wistful flights of nostalgia – which is, after all, what collecting toy soldiers is partly about. Perusal of Britains' catalogues over the years, however, reveals that the firm managed to maintain a remarkably competitive price level for products which were, indisputably, of high quality. Alfred Britain told some of the story in 1910 when interviewed for publication: 'The Germans either made soldiers solid, in

The British Indian Army provided much scope and colour for Britains, although the cavalry was usually a basic figure repainted to suit different regiments. These are Skinner's Horse, issued, like most cavalry, in sets of five.

which case the figure never had the proportionate breadth and thickness; or else, if they made them hollow, they had to do it in two pieces and solder them together. That meant another man's work for each piece; whilst if they made them solid, it meant using twice the amount of lead. So we were able to undersell them. . . .'

Prices changed little until the First World War. Prior to 1914 sets of eight infantry or five cavalry were commonly one shilling, no matter what the subject matter of the box. A Britains' price list shortly after the turn of the century offered the Royal Horse Artillery gun team for six shillings and the band of the Life Guards (12 pieces) for 5s 6d, both comparatively expensive sets considering you could have bought the imaginative and attractive mountain artillery, with pack gun, mules, men and officer, for 2s 6d and the naval landing party, with eight-man team, officer, limber and gun, for the same price. Astonishingly, more than 30 years later, in 1938, the RHA had risen only just over 50 per cent in price, to 9s 9d; by then it included five outriders, but no seated men on gun and limber; the band of the Life Guards was similarly up, to 9s.

What makes fascinating reading in the 1938 price list is the cost of some items which were then relatively expensive, but which today command little compared with others that could have been bought new much more cheaply. The answer often lay in the cost of labour and materials needed to manufacture these more pricy items. Take, for example, the splendid 4.7 naval gun, mounted on wheels for land warfare, a Britains' issue that was made in such large quantities that today even the earliest versions are sometimes sold at auction in lots of two or more together, and it is regarded as one of the more 'un-rare' of Britains' treasures.

It was first issued, without number, about 1905, recalling the honours won by this gun when offloaded by bluejackets of the British cruisers *Terrible*, *Monarch*, *Doris* and *Powerful* in the Boer War of 1899–1902. Britain's army had been found sadly lacking in heavy artillery, and the 4.7 made up some of this deficiency.

27 Britain's Highlanders, in standing, kneeling and lying positions, lend themselves magnificently to the formation of the famous British fighting square. Those lying with feet apart are the later, corrected versions and less valuable than the early, incorrect version with feet placed close together. Kneeling and standing officers hold binoculars in their movable arms.

28 Collectors know them fondly as 'ancient Britains'. The Dragoon's age is evident in his strip of tin for a sword and his clumsily modelled horse with 'one ear'. The Grenadier Guardsmen reveal their vintage by their oval bases and the awkward way in which they hold their volleying rifles.

29 In superb condition are both soldiers and box belonging to this Britains' set of Drums and Bugles of the Line. The box lid contains an informative note about the history and meaning of the lace on the drummer's tunic.

30 Britains' colourful Indian infantry (*from the left*): 2nd Bombay Native Infantry, 7th Bengal Infantry and 1st Madras Native Infantry.

31 Ever topical, Britains brought out these charging Japanese troops after Japan had gone to war with Russia in 1904. Strangely, the company never updated the uniforms, even in post-Second World War times when Japan had played a major part in international affairs. By that time, of course, they were no longer in the catalogue.

32 Classic encounter in the desert between the French Foreign Legion and Arabs. In the thirties Britains gave the Legion immense additional firepower in the form of the light machine gun, borrowed from the French line infantry set.

33 The camel-mounted Arab, toting a long barrelled rifle, was a magnificent addition to Britains' desert denizens. Among collectors he commands a figure in keeping with his lordly stature.

34 Britains' Royal Engineers pontoon section came in this review version or in service dress. Because the latter sold nowhere near as well as the colourful variety, fewer sets were made, and are therefore rarer and more valuable today. Most valuable of all is a version with the riders wearing steel helmets.

35 The first of
Britains' Egyptian army
models owed their
appearance to public
interest in the
'pacification of the
Sudan', culminating in
the Battle of
Omdourman at the end
of the nineteenth
century. Here are the
Egyptian infantry at
attention, the cavalry
and the camel corps.
Britains reissued
Egyptians at the time
of Suez.

36 Newly landed from
the swimming pool at
the Palais Mendoub in
Tangier, a Britains'
naval shore battery is
led into action by
sword-waving petty
officer. The gun was
the one used by the
mountain artillery.

37 What a little imagination and conversion skill can do: Major Henry Harris made this landing party of the Boer War support ship, *HMS Terrible*, from a Britains' 4.7 naval gun (correct), a Royal Horse Artillery limber, and non-military cattle. The result is a stunningly attractive group.

38 They might have met in khaki in the field, but such an encounter between Turkish lancers and the 10th Bengal Lancers in review order is extremely unlikely. Nevertheless, Britains' two highly popular sets make an attractive picture.

39 A new perspective on Britains' Royal Horse Guards – The Blues – in winter dress. In summer review order, The Blues had been the set numbered 2 in Britains' catalogue.

40 Sudanese infantry at the trail, with dusky faces and alarmingly prominent eyeballs, a trap that Britains' painting ladies seemed to fall into whenever they had to paint anything but an Anglo-Saxon or European face.

41 In the thirties when the shadow of a real war, fought in drab service khaki, loomed, Britains' Highlanders such as these Gordons continued to be best sellers. Nevertheless, Britains was embarking on a whole new series of mechanized transport and khaki clad troops to man it.

42 Typical of Britains' 'new modern army' of the late thirties were these anti-aircraft defence troops and equipment, comprising range finder, sound locator, spotter and chair, light anti-aircraft gun, and a heavier one mounted on a magnificent articulated lorry with lockers and cab doors that opened.

43 More of Britains' hardware which spanned the period between two wars. The gunners in puttees and flat caps were superseded by a steel-helmeted version. The heavy howitzer soldiered on, with alterations, until the end of 1980 before finally being pensioned off from Britains' sales lists.

44 A collector, complaining that Britains were stilted, commented that even the wounded seemed to be lying at attention. Nevertheless, the Royal Army Medical Corps produced by the firm was a colourful and fast-selling line. The senior medical officers never lost their oval or round bases, even when the vast majority of Britains' army went over to square or rectangular.

45 In various versions, the Royal Horse Artillery, and its companion set, the Royal Field Artillery, sold in vast quantities. Early versions had gunners seated on limber and gun; when they were removed, Britains compensated with outriders and officer as in this example.

Right

46 Among the later models and some of the best to come from Britains, three ski-troopers glide over a snowfield of cartridge paper, polystyrene and bicarbonate of soda.

47 Troops, bandsmen and mascot of the Fort Henry Guard of Canada. On the right are two members of the Canadian 89th Regiment. All were produced in Britains' closing years before the manufacture of lead toy soldiers ceased and the company went over entirely to diecast and plastic.

48 & 49 Contrast in styles between the
civilian lines of two makers and two countries:
one hunt group is early twentieth century,
modelled in flat form by a German maker,
and the other is a product of Britains sold
after the Second World War. The latter is
entitled 'The Meet'; to get a fox, you had to
buy the companion set, the 'Full Cry'.

50 In shell-pocked field, wounded Germans (composition figures mainly by Lineol) seek help from doctors and nurses as a tinplate clockwork ambulance by an unknown German maker stands by. Both Lineol and Elastolin were renowned for their lifelike poses.

Right

51 Camouflaged against the dining room wallpaper, a Lineol squad shoulders its bridging pontoon, while Elastolin shock troops paddle their rubber boat across a table top river. How many toy soldiers have campaigned in similar environments?

52 The clockwork searchlight truck, with headlamps and searchlight wired for battery powered illumination; and the flak trailer come from Hausser (Elastolin). So, too, do the riflemen and machine-gunners. Amid them a shell bursts, fired by the rival firm of Lineol.

53 Hausser, the parent factory of Elastolin soldiers, produced troops and vehicles in the livery of countries other than Germany. This British field ambulance and mobile kitchen unit dates from the inter-war years. Wheeled trolleys for horses, scorned by 'lead soldier men', were typical of the company's models.

54 Seated in the Islamic splendour of the Palais Mendoub, which houses the *Forbes* Collection in Tangier, a composition musician – possibly of German origin – plies his trade. He is one of a seated orchestra of ten men, modelled in 65mm scale.

Similar guns were used to advantage in the First World War in France, Italy and Serbia and it was not until after the war that it was phased out as a regular land weapon.

The Britains' model, catalogued as number 1264 in 1933* and renumbered as 9730 in the general reorganization of numeration in 1962, was an immediate success as it was capable of firing with commendable accuracy: it features prominently in the H.G. Wells book on basic war-gaming, *Little Wars*. It was nearly eight inches long, an impressive-looking weapon amid a corps of lead troops and sailors, just as the original 16-footer must have been in the field. It is surprising that Britains never issued with it a team of oxen, the type of motive power traditionally employed by the Royal Navy in the Boer War. (This omission has been attended to in the *Forbes* Collection with a splendid ox-drawn gun from HMS *Terrible*, a conversion by Major Henry Harris.) As to price, Britains' 4.7 – a feat of miniature engineering – was expensive in 1938, at 3s 3d, when sets of infantry and cavalry could be bought at exactly half the price (even with the outbreak of war they rose to only 2s).

Also relatively expensive was the block-busting 18-inch howitzer of the breech-loading process, on tractor wheels, at 8s 3d. Undoubtedly a unique and highly specialized piece of mechanism, the howitzer soared to 15s 6d when it was packaged as number 211 and accompanied by a ten-horse drawn team. For less than that price you could have bought a 42-piece set of the medical corps, consisting of hospital marquee, doctors, nurses, stretcher bearers and wounded, Army Service Corps waggon and ambulance waggon, each with its team of horses.

When values are projected to the present day, the howitzer's original cost stands out even more as an oddity. For its price you could have bought no fewer than *four* Britains' monoplanes, which are today collectors' pieces that far outstrip the gun in value. It was also noticeably dearer than the 14-inch wingspan working model of a Short flying boat, an aircraft which would 'fly' along stretched wire with propellors whirling. One of these models today commands easily 20 times the collector price of a howitzer.

The costliest item in the 1938 catalogue was a 73-piece presentation box at £2, containing the Royal Artillery, Life Guards, 17th Lancers, Royal Welch Fusiliers, Royal Scots Greys, a band of the line, Gordon Highlanders and general officer. At only a shilling cheaper (making its price about $10 at the then exchange rate) was a 73-piece box of US soldiers, sailors and marines, one of the sets of American forces that occupied more than three pages in the catalogue. Cheapest item in the book was a tent at a penny.

CHAPTER 18 BOOM YEARS AND WAR

The thirties found Britains extended to full capacity, the undisputed masters of the world's toy soldier markets. In Germany the hollow-cast intruders fared well against the home-produced, expensive solids, even in Dresden, the birthplace of Heydes, although the children of the Third Reich quickly switched their allegiance to the composition products of Elastolin and Lineol, the German makers who cashed in on the military and political panoply of the new regime. In the United States there was only the barest of competition from dimestore soldiery, which

---

*Why the gun remained un-numbered for so long, simply known as '4.7 inch naval gun', is one of those mysteries that makes the study of Britains interesting.

undersold the British exports but could nowhere near match them in quality; in stores like Macy's of New York and Marshall Field's of Chicago Britains' US Marine Corps, West Point Cadets and Doughboys were as familiar as Guards and Highlanders in Harrods' of London or Lewis's of Manchester. By the end of the decade when war once more confronted the British toy soldier industry with a question of survival, Britains' catalogue was the fattest ever, with hundreds of choices that ranged from the scarlet-coated battalions and squadrons of an earlier century to the mechanized 'new army' of the present day.

As it had done ever since the days of the Gamage's Life Guards, the firm wrote history in the sets it issued in the thirties. An example was Abyssynia in 1935. When Mussolini invaded Haile Selassie's landlocked country in an action which aroused universal condemnation and brought the pitifully impotent ire of the League of Nations upon his head, Britains moved fast to take advantage of topicality.

The uniforms represented in models of the Italian army were so up to date that Mussolini's war department had initiated them only the year before. The secret lay in a clever but simple piece of intelligence work by the high command in Lambton Road. The firm merely copied designs from a coloured-plate booklet issued by the Italian propaganda machine, proud to show off Rome's new legions. With its help, Britains was able to produce excellent figures of Italian infantry in shrapnel-proof helmets and in colonial service dress, each soldier with his tunic collar open showing a black shirt, symbol of the Fascists. For the first time also, colourful *Carabinieri* were added to the list.

Selassie's heroic and desperate stand, symbolized by the image of spears against tanks, was recognized by the introduction of his royal bodyguard and of tribesmen. The bodyguard was an unusual set at attention in green uniforms, peak caps and puttees and with bare feet. The tribesmen were disappointingly pedestrian, marching with ancient rifles at the slope. At a time when most British newspapers were splashed with pictures of a weak and backward nation suffering the onslaughts of modern artillery and poison gas, all the Abyssinian war sets were an instant sell-out. Three of them were re-issued after the Second World War – the tribesmen, the Italians in shrapnel-proof helmets and the *Carabinieri*.

The world focus was soon to move to a new war, and another prelude to the global conflict: the Spanish Civil War. Here, surprisingly, Britains' reaction was to ignore the new outbreak of hostilities, possibly for a combination of reasons. Earlier wars had provided clear-cut issues that defined the lines between 'baddies' and 'goodies'; no such options were open in the Spanish war with its mix of ideologies and the intervention on opposing sides of international fascism and communism. Secondly, Dennis Britain, appointed managing director in 1935, the year before the civil war and nearly two years after his father's death, might have expected, like most people outside Spain, that the conflict was going to be a short-lived affair, nothing like the bloody, three-year struggle that it turned out to be. The third reason for Britains' indifference to Spain was probably the most telling: the firm was already engaged on a punishing programme of production which, apart from extraneous orders such as the Cadbury Cubs, involved eventually a commitment to a huge range of the United Kingdom 'Modern Army'. In the event, collectors of Britains have been robbed of the chance to enjoy colourful combatants of the Spanish Civil War such as *Guardia Civil*, Foreign Legion, Moorish *Regulares* and members of the International Brigade. The firm's sole incursion into Iberian military matters has remained the Spanish infantry and cavalry of the Cuban war of 1898.

At home, royalty dominated the news for prolonged periods in the thirties, notably the death of George V, the accession of Edward VIII, the traumatic abdication crisis, and the coronation of George VI in 1937. Britains, who had not been quick enough off the mark for George V's coronation, was better prepared for

George VI and a splendid State Coach, with its team of Windsor Greys and the King and Queen as passengers, was a ready seller, priced at 8s 6d (in the 1938 catalogue), only threepence more than the heavy howitzer. The coach was, of course, reissued in the fifties for the coronation of Queen Elizabeth II, the regalia of royal office being transferred to the hands of the female incumbent of the vehicle on this occasion. In 1953 a free leaflet explained, with diagrams, how the central part of the coronation procession could be constructed from various Britains' sets, including Yeomen of the Guard, footmen, Sovereign's Escort of the Household Cavalry, attendant bands and infantry, and Royal Marines and Irish Guards at the present to line the route.

A few rare and valuable State Coaches exist from the mid-thirties which were made for the coronation that never took place – that of Edward VIII, who quit the throne to marry Wallis Simpson. They are recognizable by the solitary figure occupying the coach's seat, his crowning robes spread fully out (each of the other two versions contains monarch and consort). For Britains, the abdication meant a hasty rethink, the withdrawal of a line already in production and a new design to accommodate Edward's younger brother and sister-in-law.

Meanwhile, in the run-up to 1939, the United Kingdom was recruiting for its 'new army'. Posters that were to be seen up and down the land on the walls of army recruiting offices were reproduced in miniature to decorate barrack buildings and guardhouses produced by the firm of Britains as part of its Modern Army series. The company was into khaki with a vengeance. Anti-aircraft defence, with sound

Britains' khaki had been on the scene since before the 1914–18 war – and not always with commercial success. In time for a new war in 1939 this veteran transport – despatch rider, and ambulance and Service Corps waggons – had surrendered pride of place to equipment symbolizing the United Kingdom's 'new modern army'. The mechanized units can be seen in colour in photographs 42 and 43.

locators, range finders, spotters in chairs, guns and barrage balloons, fore-shadowed the nature of the coming war with Germany. Air raid precaution teams appeared in the familiar crimson boxes. There were firefighters in all-enveloping white flameproof suits. Britains' army and civilians were being called to war service. And in time, of course, that is precisely what happened to the company, as had happened in the First World War.

For nearly two years after the outbreak of war in 1939 the firm existed on a severely curtailed production schedule. Material was available only for export – and that meant principally to the North American continent. The quality of figures suffered from thin metal and paint that was not up to standard. Skilled hands were called up into the forces. By 1942, Britains had gone completely over to war production, having sent out its final price list to customers, proclaiming that 'our goods' were 'made in England entirely by British labour.'

Whereas shrapnel balls had been Britains' major contribution in the earlier war, the firm's role was now to manufacture zinc diecastings for mines and bombs, and parts of fuses for shells. Again, the men and women whose occupation had been the making of toys switched their skills to munitions. Britains' wartime experience, however, did not stand in isolation as a period of stagnation in its commercial fortunes. It was the wartime necessity that impelled Dennis Britain to go out and buy diecasting machines that laid the foundation for the firm's post-war expansion into diecast toys. The future had already been anticipated as early as the late thirties when he had examined the possibility of making soldiers from plastic – 'but at the time the materials available were too expensive.'

For Dennis Britain, however, both toy soldiers and alternative production had to wait. There was a war to be fought. He joined the Royal Air Force and became a specialist in night fighting. He would like to have been a pilot, but was deemed too old. Instead he became an air gunner, flying in Beaufighters and Mosquitos. During 20 months of flying service he became expert in the handling of radio-based interception devices, shot down five German bombers, and was awarded the Distinguished Flying Cross. Following his successes, he was put in charge of radar navigation school and finally served in New Delhi as chairman of the Asian Establishment War Committee. When war ended he left the RAF as a wing-commander, and returned to set about enlarging his company's range and to develop its export side until eventually it was to account for 60 per cent of all sales (his services to exports subsequently led to his decoration as an Officer of the British Empire).

For the time being, however, there was no question of anything *but* exports. Lead was available only on licence and only if the soldiers made from it were sold abroad. So, for 18 months, all new production went overseas and anything sold in Britain came from existing stocks.

CHAPTER **19** **THE END OF LEAD**

The war era produced a few issues of Britains which are now scarce and high in collector esteem. 'Dad's Army' – the Home Guard, which had started as the Local Defence Volunteers to bolster the United Kingdom's meagre defences in the dark days of Dunkirk – found an honourable place in the catalogue. They marched with rifles slung on their shoulders and wore forage caps, a uniformly military-looking squad, unlike the real thing with its variety of heights, ages and girths; the miniature Home Guards were, after all, merely a British infantryman given a different kind of rifle arm and label on the box.

Similarly, British flyers, pressed into German uniforms, became Luftwaffe pilots, eight to a box, to provide the enemy for the Battle of Britain. There was to be no updating of the machines they flew, however. Britains' monoplanes and biplanes were never modernized: they remained the somewhat underscaled relics of the inter-war period, although the army's wheeled equipment underwent subsequent modernization in the form of a Centurion tank, a Jeep-like Austin Champ and an intricate and convincing model of a 155-millimetre gun, among other developments.

With peace, the United Kingdom's allies were afforded recognition. A set of 'Snowdrops', the American military police, was issued, partly because they had been a familiar feature of life in British cities, towns and villages during the wartime alliance – although British 'MPs' were never thus honoured as a separate boxed set – and partly because all eyes were perforce on the export market, which was strongest across the Atlantic. With Russia's heroism and victories fresh in mind, and the Cold War still over the horizon, Britains brought out a greatcoated Red Army guardsman, marching with slung rifle and a set of cavalry at the halt to supplement our old friends, the Cossacks; of these two new issues, the one was a Grenadier Guard with new headgear and rifle arm, the other a reincarnation of British standing cavalry. Allies nearer home, the Danes, were accorded the salute of an entirely new figure of the Livgarde, the royal foot guard, an issue whose subsequent collector value was underwritten by its comparatively short catalogue life: it was off the list by 1960.

With the lifting of lead restrictions and the opening of the home market within 18 months, the way was open for an exciting programme of new issues under the direction of the returned war hero, Dennis Britain, who had inherited from his father a flair for inventiveness and experiment. Although Britains was to prosper even more than before, however, there was never again to be the huge variety of production that had made the immediate prewar catalogues such bumper publications.

The year 1949 saw the birth of one of the firm's most elegant military figures,

The alliance with Russia and its victories over Hitler's Germany were recognized in these greatcoated Red Army Guards (and other issues) which complemented the popular Cossacks who had been on the scene for many years. Topicality was a strong marketing virtue of Britains.

number 2037, a ski trooper. He was poised, as if in motion, his ski poles held behind him. Dressed overall in white – a light grey in one version which was issued in single 'Picture Packs' between 1954 and 1959, he carried a slung rifle which was plugged into a hole in his shoulder, and pack equipment on his back.

By 1954, Britains' customers had a total of nearly 400 catalogue sets from which to choose – much fewer than the prewar heyday but almost fourfold the number that had been available in 1947. Of the firm's foreign rivals, Heyde had been bombed into oblivion; so too, presumably, had Lineol; Elastolin and the French makers like Mignot were still picking up the pieces and making tentative steps towards full production again; the United States, with its diffuse toy soldier industry, was ripe for export opportunities.

Britains' response to the challenge was a range of new issues that was decidedly catholic (and in one case Catholic: the Papal Guard of the Vatican, a most attractive set of bloomer-clad figures holding halberds). It embraced items as different from each other as a new steel-helmeted Red Army infantryman, holding his rifle across the chest Russian-fashion, a Wild West 'prairie schooner', or covered waggon, equipped with two aged pioneers, and a strangely solid-looking Algerian Spahi mounted on a horse that appeared too clumsy to come from a Britains stable. The Spahi did not appear until 1958 and, again, he is rare because there was not time to produce many before lead production ceased.

That time was now fast approaching. Britains' directors were facing their most critical period of reassessment and decision. As Dennis Britain has explained, prewar experiments with plastic were shelved because of the expense of materials. Pressures on Britains and other makers to seek an alternative to metal in the post-war years were twofold: there was the economic problem of rising material and labour costs and the expense of shipping lead goods in an expanding export market; and there was the social, moral and governmental attitudes to the use of lead in toys. Dennis Britain said:

In the early 1950s we decided to start producing some models in plastic. Polythene had become available at a reasonable price but there were problems in paint adherence. Lead soldiers were becoming too expensive as a commercial proposition, and so, with the advent of suitable grades of PVC, which has no paint problem, we decided to give up all production of lead soldiers after 1967.* Another reason for this decision was because, by injecting plastic under pressure, finer detail is obtained, limited under-cuts can be got out of a mould, and parts can be assembled after being injected in the required colour, thus saving a lot of hand painting.

Answering a collector's query about the cessation of lead production in 1967, Britain wrote: 'We are toy manufacturers, and there has been a big public outcry against lead in toys.' On the subject of the risk, he was unequivocal: 'Although we never heard of a single case of poisoning either among our employees or customers over a period of 60 years, we bowed to public opinion.'

In private conversation he has expanded on this theme. It is the oxides in lead that are responsible for poisoning, not the lead itself, he points out, and argues that the whole question of lead poisoning was fraught with emotional overtones. 'We had a caster in the 1930s who complained of stomach pains. His doctor asked, "Where do you work?" "Britains" was the reply. "Ah ah," said the doctor. "That's it. Lead poisoning." He just jumped to the conclusion. We sent the man to a specialist for exhaustive tests, and the results were negative, nothing to do with his work and lead.'

He recalls efforts in the inter-war years to ensure that the paint used on the firm's models was safe. 'We made our own spirit paint, even grinding up the paint pigment itself inside the factory. For the mixture that was used for Guardsmen's

*Coincidentally, the Statutory Regulations 1967 forbade the manufacture of any toy soldier having a coat of paint which contained lead.

tunics we used a genuine, rich vermillion. Because of opinion from some quarters we changed the entire paint process to guarantee our colours were lead free.' Painting, of course, was always a highly supervised area of production at Britains, understandably so when one learns that up to ten changes of colour or brush might be needed on a single foot figure.

Britain is on record in 1967 as saying: 'Believe me, it has been just as sad for me as it has been for many collectors that we had to give up production of lead soldiers.' Sad though it was for the collectors, the decision enhanced the value of their armies overnight and led to the new industry of trading in and auctioning of lead soldiers that was to reach fever pitch in the seventies and eighties. In the Britains' factory, now moved to Blackhorse Lane in Walthamstow, London, it meant that old skills were now being applied to new methods of production.

According to Britains, in a paper on the subject prepared for public relations purposes, research behind modern plastic figures and diecast vehicles is just as exhaustive as that undertaken in the heyday of the lead soldier. Whereas before, the modeller would resort to old prints, histories of the regiment and – in the case of a British soldier – to the War Office (the embassy's military attaché if it were a representative of a foreign army to be modelled), Britains' researchers now go to the companies who manufacture the motorcycles to be reproduced in miniature, to the makers of farm machinery, to authentic sources of scale drawings for details of sophisticated war machinery.

Hundreds of requests a year flow in to the company for particular models to be made. These are carefully filed and categorized, weighed against requests and information received from the firm's agents in various countries, from retailers and other sources, and discussed at periodic meetings of directors and the sales staff. Similar requests have been considered, and sometimes met, by Britains ever since the firm went into toy soldiers. The criterion to be met was whether the production order would be large enough to make it worthwhile for the company to tool up for the commission.

Will Britains ever go back again to lead soldiers as a purely collectors' range, priced accordingly? Most unlikely, is the view of Dennis Britain. 'If we did start production again, the secondhand value of our soldiers would crash overnight. But this is not a reason that influences our decision,' he is on record as having said. In fact, in 1973 the firm issued a new metal soldier, a model of the Scots Guards in zinc and aluminium. Handpainted by outworkers, the figure was regarded by collectors with mild curiosity. It was cheap but, disappointingly, about a quarter of an inch too tall to be used effectively for conversion purposes among 54-millimetre figures.

One of Britains' most finely executed wheeled models was the Royal State Landau and its team of six Windsor Greys, produced for the coronation of Queen Elizabeth II and containing the royal couple. Behind are late versions of the Life Guards, William Britain's first figure.

At Blackhorse Lane, where, in modern single-storey factory premises, torrents of plastic sheep pour out of moulding machines cheek by jowl with diecasting equipment engaged on the manufacture of super-sophisticated vehicles, there is little tangible evidence of Britains' great toy soldier past. A small number of sets has been preserved, among them a miniscule (one centimetre high) group of guardsmen, made to scale for the nursery of the luxurious doll's house presented to Queen Mary and now a national relic. Britains' heritage lies hidden away in locked storerooms – the complete set of moulds that produced the biggest toy army the world has ever known. 'Just think what we might do to the market if we started using them again,' says Dennis Britain with a chuckle.

CHAPTER **20** MISTAKES MAKE MONEY

As in philately, the unusual commands a premium in toy soldier collecting. Just as a mistake in printing can boost the value of a set of postage stamps, so can a set of soldiers gain in collector interest if it has been the subject of a *temporary* aberration of uniform design or some other aspect of military styling. The word 'temporary' is stressed because there are certain base rules in this game of error and rarity. To qualify, the model or range must have been corrected within a limited period of time, thus confining the 'wrong' versions to comparatively few in number.

Various well-known howlers committed by Continental manufacturers when turning their attention to the British army can, therefore, hardly be classed as rarities for the simple reason that they were so common. Heyde of Germany frequently put the Life Guards on brown, instead of black, horses, a crime which William Britain's commercial acumen was quick to exploit when he remarked in 1915 that any 'English boy knows better than that!' In Madrid the same mistake was made in the thirties by Palomeque, whose ladies of the paint shop seem to have been given a remarkably free rein to exercise their own indulgence in the matter of colours. Another Spanish maker, Capell, the successor to Casanellas in 1925, mounted Royal Scots Greys on dark horses, despite the obvious indication inherent in the regiment's name. No one would blame a non-Scot for losing his way in the strange world of tartans, kilts and bagpipes, therefore it was no surprise to find Heinrichsen's mounted Highland officers wearing kilts instead of trews, and both Heyde and Mignot manufacturing quasi-Scots with ludicrously 'thin' bearskins instead of the forbidding, shaggy headgear that topped the 'thin red line' at Balaclava. Heyde went astray when delving into the mysteries of Africa and the Wild West; thus Red Indians and Kaffirs often appear interchangeable, and the inclusion of warriors wielding bolasses of the South American Pampas contributes a note of piquancy to a North American buffalo hunt – a set highly valuable because of its rarity rather than the mistakes it encompasses. Other Heyde aberrations involved basic flaws of design rather than slips in accuracy: a magnificent group of large-scale British Camel Corps in the *Forbes* Collection suffers from such a fault – the ponderous bodies of the camels, added to the riders' weight are too much for the animals' slender legs and the result is that the figures need constant adjustment to counteract buckling legs and bellies that scrape the sand.

Britains, too, made mistakes. But the firm's regard of accuracy usually led it to correct them when they were pointed out, and this policy has left a rich and curious legacy of rarities that has contributed interest and reward to the business of collecting this maker's wares. The British Rifle regiments seem to have been a particularly troublesome area for the firm. One of the very early issues was the Rifle Brigade in 1897, a formation which Britains made marching with movable arms carrying rifles at the slope. Someone – it might have been the regiment, or an old soldier – informed the company that the Rifle Brigade *never* carried their rifles this way; at the trail would have been acceptable, but *never* at the slope. The set was withdrawn (oddly enough, not until 1918), but comparatively few had been made and those that survive attract some of the highest bids for sets of infantry at present-day auctions.

In 1899 a Britains' figure of the King's Royal Rifle Corps appeared. He was running, carrying his rifle at the trail, and he had a rather prominent chest as a result of some esoteric moulding; this physical feature, common to a couple of other contemporary sets, has coined the familiar phrase 'pigeon chested' which denotes to a collector an early model. His headgear, alas, was out of date, as Britains were quickly informed by the military *cognoscenti*. He was wearing the spiked helmet instead of the rifleman's raccoon cap to which the regiment had switched a few years earlier. The mistake was swiftly remedied – and another candidate entered the department of valuable rarities.

Wrong and rare, too, was the South Australian Lancer, produced in time for Queen Victoria's diamond jubilee in 1897. First in review order, then in khaki with red plastron on his chest, he aroused no controversy over his uniform for the simple reason there was no such regiment. Did Britains have in mind the Adelaide Lancers, the only unit that might fit the bill? No one knows. Nevertheless, he soldiered through the Boer War, survived the coronations of Edward VII and George VI and vanished with the coming of the Great War, a dashing anachronism.

A basic error of another kind – anatomical position – was that of set number 118, the Gordon Highlanders lying firing, issued in time for 1901 date-stamping. These were the troops said to have been planned originally in khaki and then put into bright tunics and tartans for more effective commercial appeal. They lay with feet elegantly placed together, a minor feat of sculpture, but one which brought ridicule from old soldiers. Try lying like that and discharging a heavy rifle, they pointed out, and you might roll over with the force of the recoil. At the least, the position would afford little stability for accurate aim. Britains was aware of the problem but did nothing about it until the thirties when a new figure, with legs spread wide apart, was introduced. In the meantime, so many of the Gordons and other Highland regiments were made in the prone position with crossed feet that they can hardly be described as rare. Nevertheless a 'wrong' lying Highlander is worth more today than a 'right' one.

Complainants who wrote to Britains were not always right, however. The firm has on file a letter from the British military attaché in Washington taking issue over a figure, he said, of a Coldstream Guardsman who was wrongly wearing the plume on the left side of his busby. Britains demurred. The model was not a Coldstream, but an accurately painted member of the Governor General's Foot Guards of Canada.

What is perhaps one of the strangest cases of an incorrect uniform – the **mystery of the Polish infantry** – was not a mistake at all but a matter of commercial expediency on Britains' part, according to American collector Donald A. Wollheim, who has researched the affair and reported his findings and conclusions in *Old Toy Soldier Newsletter*. The plot is as murky as the background against which it was laid, the gathering clouds of war in Europe in the two or three years leading up to the outbreak in September 1939.

Britains' flair for topicality is well known, although there were notable lapses: its Chinese infantry, based on the native protagonists in the Boxer Rebellion, did not, for example, appear until 1925, some 25 years after the uprising. Nevertheless, the firm was mostly on the ball when it came to predicting popular demand for troops engaged in current events. Therefore it is no surprise to see that a set of Polish infantry, number 1856, was issued in 1939, for it must have been evident to the directors in Lambton Road, as to everyone else, that Poland would be next on Hitler's list after Austria and Czechoslovakia.

The Poles' bodies were patently from an old set, the German infantry, marching with slope arms. Their heads and brimless, basin-like helmets were the same as those worn by the Italian infantry, issued at the time of Mussolini's invasion of Abyssinia in 1935. So far, so good: Poland had adopted this type of helmet in the thirties, after abandoning a French-type *casque*. But Britains' uniforms were a blue-grey colour, completely unlike anything worn by the army in Poland at that time. In fact, Polish uniforms were khaki. How could Britains make such an elementary mistake? Wollheim's conjecture is that it didn't.

He argues thus: Britains in the late thirties was in one of its 'keeping-up-with-current-events outlooks', and had its eyes on Czechoslovakia which appeared to be the next theatre of news after Austria. Although the army wore khaki, there was a highly visible National Guard which sported the more distinctive colour of blue-grey – and Czech helmets were of the rimless kind as worn by the Italians, Dutch and Danes, among others. Had the 'Polish infantry' appeared with the label, 'Czech National Guard', it would have made sense. And the conjecture is that this

A set produced for the diamond jubilee of Queen Victoria in 1897 was the South Australian Lancers, now extremely valuable because of its rarity. It has an added cachet because it was a mistake: no such regiment existed.

is precisely what Britains at first intended. But events – in the form of the 1938 Munich Pact which ended Czechoslovakia's independence – moved too quickly. As Wollheim explains:

Britains found itself with several thousands of blue-grey soldiers (intended as Czechs) and nowhere to go with them. Some genius on the sales staff may then have come up with the well-known belief that Poland was going to be the next critical point. So just relabel the boxed as Polish and rush them out. Who would know the difference? And so they did. And once having made the decision, they were not going to correct it.

The story does not end there. There are two other Britains' sets – both issued in 1939 – from the 'Polish' casting. One is number 1837, Argentine infantry, the other number 1850, Netherlands' infantry. The Argentinians were painted a brownish khaki, which is more or less correct, but their rimless helmets were wrong, as the Argentine army wore a German-style helmet; how did that come about when, if faced with an order for Argentinians, all that Britains needed to have done was repaint the casts of the German infantry? On the other hand, the Dutch Britains, in field grey, were acceptably uniformed and helmeted.

Wollheim's theory is that in 1938 Britains had, in fact, been painting soldiers khaki for a genuine projected Polish set, one that was overtaken by the necessity for a sudden outlet for the redundant Czechs. What to do with these – probably no more than a few hundred – was solved by calling them Argentinians and trying to do a deal with a Buenos Aires importer. It took time to make such a deal, however, and in the meantime war broke out, and the hybrid Argentinians trickled into United Kingdom toyshops.

The firm still had many more casting that had not been painted. It decided to make them Dutch and paint them field grey, with the conviction that Holland would remain neutral in the war as it had done in 1914. The potential export market crumbled, however, when Hitler's panzers rolled over the Low Countries in a few days of 1940. Those Dutch toy soldiers which had been finished went into home shops and production was soon to stop, anyway, because of the war. Britains learned that topicality can be a very ephemeral thing. And collectors gained three more rare goals to seek.

This chapter on mistakes must inevitably close on the treasonable affair of the Queen's moustache. Britains' painting instructions, the story goes, used to decree moustaches for officers – an order fulfilled by a thin, deft stroke of the paint brush. In some sets the officer achieves distinction by being the only mounted figure, therefore it was easy for some of the older women painters to associate a figure on horseback with commissioned status. When Queen Elizabeth II appeared, riding side-saddle her famous horse Winston in the fifties, it was the days of outworkers. Some examples of the figure came back to the paint depots bearing a moustache, passed unnoticed in the departmental scrutiny, and went out for sale. What had happened, we like to believe, is that some woman or women, faced with the boringly repetitive regimen of painting hundreds, maybe thousands, of figures, had reasoned that mounted figure = officer = moustache, and decorated the Queen's top lip accordingly. Whether this is true or not, such hirsute queens do exist – and bring a price accordingly higher when they change hands in collecting circles.

Mistakes were not confined to figures. The Cossacks, first issued for the Russo-Japanese war in 1904, had their label updated by artist Fred Whisstock after the Revolution when Russia became the 'Union of Soviet Socialist Republics'.

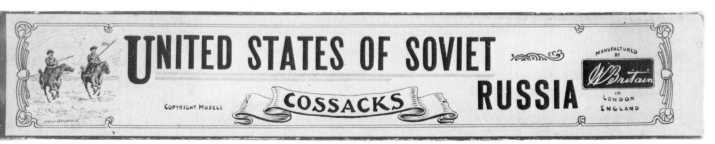

With the potential evident in a huge English-speaking export market, it is not surprising that Britains paid considerable attention to the production of toy soldiers of American interest. Because of various considerations, however, such as the need to establish a trading base and range of products, and the intervention of the First World War, exports to North America were not a major factor in the firm's fortunes until the early twenties. Nevertheless, the first issue of American soldiers was made as early as 1898 – in such a hurry that it became the subject of one of those design 'hiccups' that made for rarity. The story behind the set explains why 'ancient Britains' are such a fascinating field for the dedicated collectors of toy soldiers.

The occasion was the Spanish-American war which began with the blowing up of the battleship *Maine* in Cuba, where most of the fighting took place. William Britain's interest in representing troops engaged in the war could hardly have stemmed from considerations of exports to the United States or Spain, as his firm's effort were overwhelmingly concentrated on cementing a home market in those early days. But his shrewd sense for news values told him that the United States' new war would capture public interest in the United Kingdom, already stimulated by the climactic campaigns in the Sudan where Anglo-Egyptian forces were putting the seal on nearly two decades of intermittent warfare against first the Mahdi and then his successor, the Khalifa. That the Spanish-American war would be a very public one was ensured by the part played in it by the media, notably the press of William Randolph Hearst whose suspect manipulations have been deemed one of the causes of the conflict. At a time of rapidly increasing use of improved communications, such as the undersea cable, and the growth of popular picture papers – now using photographs to supplement the works of war artists, what was news in the United States was news in the United Kingdom.

Against this background, William Britain designed a set each of United States infantry and Spanish infantry, and numbered them 91 and 92 respectively. 'Designed' is, on reflection, hardly the word as he utilized the basic British infantry figure of the previous year, giving the American enlisted men movable arms carrying rifles at the slope, and the Spanish rifles at the trail. In each case the officer was the old fixed-arm type. Both sets were in review order, the Americans wearing dark blue tunics and light blue breeches, the Spanish in dark blue tunics and red trousers. The only physical changes needed in the moulds were in the matter of headgear. The Spaniards were given kepis. All published records hitherto accepted that the American toy soldiers were equipped from the start with western-style campaign hats. But a new entry was written into Britains' lore in the late 1970s, when a set of first version United States infantry was discovered in the attic of a London house among a late Victorian collection of lead soldiers and other toys.

Eventually, this set went to a new home in California, to grace the collection of early Britains owned by Edward Ruby. He says: 'To a collector, they were the weirdest set of Britains. I knew they were "right", I knew they were rare, but somehow I just couldn't figure out how these particular models had slipped through the records.' It was a challenge and Ruby, like a good collector, took it up and set about tracking down the origin of the figures.

There was no mystery about the box number, 91, with a delightfully decorated lid. Neither was there anything unusual about the basic uniforms and poses of the troops inside the box. They were the early type of rifles-at-the-slope men and fixed arm officer (changed in 1907 to men with rifles and bayonets at the ready and officer with sword and pistol – based on the successful City Imperial Volunteers). 'But,' says Ruby, 'can you believe it? They all wore *white helmets*!' What had happened to the slough hats? There was no question of heads having been replaced after the soldiers had been sold to the first owner; the heads were original. With his knowledge of the workings of the firm of Britains, Ed Ruby eventually divined the story behind these extremely rare soldiers and produced a solution which is immediately plausible to collectors.

When war began between the United States and Spain, Britains was eager to rush on to the market the troops of the opposing sides. As often happened, the only immediate references to uniform details were coloured military prints. Someone in the Britains' household found a picture of US troops who were then using a white, spiked dress helmet, similar to that issued to many British regiments. That was it. The American soldiers passed through the mould and the painting process only months, possibly weeks, after outbreak of war, sporting the white helmets.

It was not until the war's first pictures, both drawings and photographs, began to appear in publications like the *Illustrated London News* and the *Graphic*, that it became obvious that the common headgear of American troops fighting in Cuba was, in fact, the slouch hat of the type to be made famous by Teddy Roosevelt's Rough Riders. Britains' first attempt hadn't been a mistake, for, after all, it purported to depict Americans in review order. Nevertheless, the slouch hat so rapidly became synonymous with the US combatants that William Britain decided it was better for business that a new figure be cast wearing that headgear. In no time, the new, corrected model was on the market and the very few wearing spiked helmets were conveniently forgotten. Indeed, so limited were the manufactured numbers of the very first version that hardly any authority on Britains' soldiers has recorded them, let alone come across a set.

Britains' next venture into American military spheres was a strange production, a set which incorporated a game, and the decision to give one version an American nationality (a companion set came with Royal Lancaster Regiment figures) suggests that as early as 1907 the prospect of transatlantic markets must have crossed the minds of William and Fred Britain. The unusual – and now utterly rare – figures consisted, in the American version, of soldiers at the double, wearing dark and light blue uniforms and shakos *à la* West Point Cadets. Their rectangular bases fitted into tin slides pivoted to a board which, when tipped, caused the squad to stand up. An officer on prancing horse completed the set. This failed to survive the Great War and so rare is it today that several years' close monitoring of toy soldier auction sales on both sides of the Atlantic has failed to spot more than one appearing on the market.

It was soon to be followed by the forerunners of a popular series of issues – a group of North American Indians. In the end, Indians and cowboys were to appear, sometimes in new poses, more often in different groupings and re-boxed sets, together with tents and later a covered waggon and a rodeo display, at sporadic intervals over the next 60 years: more than 30 sets in all. Small boys everywhere loved them. They were made in millions.

Although the fascination for the West was apparent to Britains, the firm inexplicably waited until the mid-thirties before issuing what was to be another deservedly popular line: the Canadian Mounted Police in their familiar uniform of campaign hat, red tunic, blue pants with broad yellow stripe and riding boots. The Mounties had been introduced in the previous decade but only as a dull brown version in winter dress, marching at the slope. When the red-jacketed version appeared on the scene at full gallop, it was based on the late nineteenth century figure of the South African Mounted Infantry.

Canada was eventually accorded more than 20 issues, including cavalry such as the Governor General's Horse Guards and infantry such as Princess Patricia's. There were several named sets of regiments, but most were derivative of old favourites. An outstanding exception came in the closing years of lead production: it was a pioneer of the Fort Henry Guard, one of several Fort Henry and similar

Popular dollar earners for Britains in the American market were the Marine Corps (*extreme left*); their officer stands next to three examples of the US whitejackets, attractive and distinctive figures. In the foreground are US Marines by the German firm of Heyde, which also successfully penetrated the American market.

historically garbed soldiers which, until very recent times, were still being sold at the Ontario fort.

With the wartime alliance a warm and recent memory and lucrative markets beckoning across the Atlantic, Britains made its first really big push into the American military ranks in the early twenties, shortly after Dennis Britain joined the firm as a young man. The Doughboys were commemorated, so were the US Marines, sailors and cavalry. The West Point Cadets appeared in winter dress (later a summer version was produced); these were slim, boyish figures, an integral part of the American military scene, but comparatively unexciting characters.

Through the remaining years of the twenties, the thirties and again after the war, American issues poured out of the factory for a market that was now a mainstay of the company's income. There were review and combat troops, medics and artillery, American versions of the engineers' pontoon waggon, planes, autogiro and motorized transport, bands, airmen and even American girl scouts. Until the United States' forces adopted the now familiar form of helmet, the First World War 'tin hat' sufficed for both British and American models, who were, of course, both conveniently in khaki. At Britains it was often a simple matter of giving puttees a different shade of green or khaki and re-labelling the boxes for the export market, once more emphasizing the importance of the original box in collecting circles.

An obvious area of American military activity is the Civil War, and although Britains' '1862' sets were to achieve enormous popularity they were not introduced until after the Second World War. In some respect this tardiness was not surprising to collectors of Britains, for the firm made – apart from some notable exceptions – few excursions into history when deciding on new series. In the event, its Confederate and Union infantry, cavalry and artillery were based on a mixed bunch of earlier figures. Inevitably, the universally serviceable City Imperial Volunteers of the Boer War obliged with their moulds for some of the models.

By closedown in 1967, nearly 120 American sets – excluding individual Picture Packs – had appeared in the catalogues. Many were, of course, combinations of earlier issues, or simply re-issues, but the volume and variety of troops shipped across the Atlantic was evidence that Britains paid the United States more attention than any other foreign maker. On the basis of that attention was built a collector interest which is today probably even more extensive and intense than in the home country of Mr Britain.

CHAPTER **22** OVERSEAS CAMPAIGNS

Collecting Britains is today an international business. In each country where it takes place it is, no doubt, stimulated to some extent by the firm's original export push there. How many collectors there are is anyone's guess. Peter Blum, of The Soldier Shop in New York, has been quoted as estimating the United States total of collectors of *all kinds of soldiers* at something between 50 000 and 100 000. Besides the United Kingdom, United States and Canada, the main collecting countries are France, Germany, Italy, the Netherlands, South Africa, some parts of South America, Spain and Scandinavia; and, of course, countries where there are populations of dominantly British stock, notably Australia and New Zealand. Significantly, Britains' catalogues paid attention to the troops from all these areas, in varying degrees.

Earlier chapters have hailed the arrival of the French Zouaves, cuirassiers and dragoons at the time of production in the Paris factory, before the First World War; then a little later, the steel-helmeted *Poilus*; and the dashing French Colonial Spahis of Algeria, a new line of the post-Second World War era. There was, in fact, a comparatively large contingent of France's soldiers – no fewer than about 30 sets (including re-issues and combinations), more than the company fielded for the British Dominion of Canada. They included *chasseurs à cheval*, colourful *infanterie de ligne* and energetic sailors, or *matelots*, at the double, all from the French factory. About the time of the 1914 war, Turcos made their debut, merely being the Zouaves painted a grey blue colour. The *Poilus* in action, introduced after that war, were subsequently equipped with more firepower in the form of machine guns. Just before the next war the long-overdue Foreign Legion, marching at the slope, with mounted officer at the halt, were produced to complement their traditional opponents of romantic fiction, the Arabs who were old Britains' friends. When legionnaires and Arabs were combined in a large box the former had already been given the machine gun of the line infantry, which must have upset the balance of armaments between them and the spear, scimitar and musket waving Arabs.

No doubt because Belgium was a United Kingdom ally in two world wars, its soldiers were handsomely represented by Britains, having first made their appearance by the outbreak of war in 1914 in the form of greatcoated infantry and colourful *chasseur* cavalry standing at the halt. Later sets came out as infantry and cavalry in active service dress and were largely repainted existing figures, such as those of the French *Poilus*. Belgian grenadiers were borrowed from French *infanterie* and British Guards.

Britains' attention to Germany was meagre, to say the least, considering the country was always regarded as one of the major areas of export potential (in the seventies it was, in fact, the firm's largest overseas market). We have, as a result, only the German infantry marching at the slope in field grey, issued in 1931 and later the basis of several other nationalities, and the Luftwaffe pilots of the Battle of Britain – a notably miserable delegation from a country so rich in military panoply and variety. Additionally, of course, there had been two very early sets of Prussians: infantry marching at the slope and wearing *pickelhauben* headgear, and a box of magnificent hussars, all but the officer carrying lances. These were on the scene by 1908. Equally exotic were four sets of soldiers of Germany's ally, Austro-Hungary – lancers, dragoons, line infantry and foot guards. They made an all too brief blaze of colour that was snuffed out by the war that eliminated their European empire. Needless to say, both the Prussians and the Austro-Hungarians are among the rarest of Britains' products today.

Italy's representation has been described when dealing with the Abyssinian war period of history. There were, however, other notable contributions from Britains. The first was the result of one of William Britain's determined attempts to make topical capital out of a war, the conflict in Tripoli between Italy and Turkey in 1911–12. He designed review order lancers at the halt (from British 9th Lancers of 1903) and a set of marching infantry decked out, Italian style, with prominent epaulettes. Some long-lived and popular figures made a début, the feather-hatted *Bersaglieri*, carrying slung rifles. Coincidental to these sets, of course, came their enemy, Turkish infantry with a more offensive stance of rifle and bayonet at the ready.

Britains' commitment to the Netherlands was small and short-lived, consisting of just two boxes of infantry produced as a result of the Polish fiasco (Chapter 20). Find them, however, in mint, boxed condition and you have a valuable acquisition.

South Africa has a rich legacy of history left in the form of Britains' models, which is hardly surprising considering the public's pre-occupation with affairs in that part of the world during the closing decade of the nineteenth century and the opening years of the twentieth. The first sets to be issued, of course, were the Boer cavalry and infantry, whose appearance has been acknowledged elsewhere. And, although strictly home based or raised, several British army regiments came on to the market about that time because of their prominence in news despatches about the second Boer War of 1899 to 1902; they included units like the Devonshires, Gloucesters, Dublin Fusiliers, Imperial Yeomanry and CIVs. They were, it is interesting to note, not always issued because of British victories (for these were few and far between), but often followed what were in effect disastrous defeats translated into propaganda and marketing terms as desperate and heroic last stands.

As early as series number 38 in the company's lists there appeared a set of mounted figures that was remarkable on two counts: firstly, it commemorated a tragi-comic defeat of British arms – the Jameson Raid of the late 1890s – which no-one but the most jingoistic could fail to construe as a vainglorious and foolhardy venture; secondly, it led to a unique incursion by Britains into the manufacture of a model of a named military personality, Dr Jameson. (Subsequent personality figures made by the firm tended to be confined to royalty and were characterized by those produced under arrangements such as that with Madame Tussaud's waxworks.) The raid had taken place as a result of the unsettled situation left by the war of 1880–81 between Boer and Briton in the Transvaal. A gold rush in the Witwatersrand in 1886 had brought a large influx of foreigners, or *Uitlanders*, mainly British. Under the Transvaal Boers, these were being refused civil rights, including the vote, thus giving rise to angry public feeling in the Transvaal itself, in neighbouring Rhodesia and in the United Kingdom. With collusion inside the British Cabinet, a revolt was plotted by the *Uitlanders* but dissension among them led to the shelving of this plan. Notwithstanding, Dr Jameson, the administrator of Rhodesia, invaded the Transvaal from Bechuanaland with 470 mounted police, an ill-considered venture that lacked support from the *Uitlanders*. The results were ignominious surrender when the hard riding and fighting Boers surrounded him near Johannesburg on 2 January 1897, political scandal in British southern

Impelled by the initial, immediate postwar restriction of 'export only', and later by the need to consolidate world markets, Britains produced some of its best foreign issues in the years leading up to the closedown of lead production in the sixties. These splendid figures are the Swiss Papal Guard of the Vatican, with their officer.

Africa and at home, the inflaming of Boer opinion, and another step nearer to the full-scale war that came two years later. Undaunted, William Britain produced a boxed set of five at full gallop, 'Dr Jameson and the South African Mounted Infantry'. The men carried rifles. Jameson pointed a pistol at the heart of southern Africa, otherwise he had no distinguishing features to make him recognizable. Very soon his name was dropped from the box label and the trigger-happy figure became just another officer. The final irony is that the set was, in fact, nothing more than Boer cavalry in disguise.

South Africa, of course, was the home of another early issue, the Zulus, soon to be followed by a *kraal* set boxed in a background scene of the *veldt*, with incongruous palm trees and two round huts looking like upturned half-coconut shells. Then for 20 years or more South Africa was given a rest as far as new issues were concerned, while other wars intervened. In the thirties three interesting series, all of which command handsome prices in modern collector circles, appeared as the Regiment Louw Wepener, Cape Town Highlanders, and steel-helmeted infantry of the Union of South Africa defence forces. All owed their existence to earlier moulds.

A modern phenomenon in the collecting world has been a growth of interest from the direction of South America, particularly from the Argentine, Uruguay, Venezuela, Brazil, and – in Central America, Mexico. With the exception of Brazil, all these countries were catered for by Britains. Attention to the Argentine and Uruguay was first paid shortly after the First World War when, no doubt, William Britain had in mind the export potential in areas which possessed considerable expatriate British population. He produced Argentine infantry cavalry and cadets of the military school, together with parallel sets for Uruguay. To quote the British authority on Britains, author and collector L.W. Richards, in his definitive list and survey prepared for the Journal of the British Model Soldier Society:

These six boxes of the armies of the two countries of South America brought some colourful models into the shops, shakos being in abundance. They were just the thing to catch the eye and they were most popular with those who had conversions in mind. The cavalry, as usual, had their figures derived from existing models. . . . The Uruguayan cavalry were in blue and the Argentine French grey. . . All the foot figures wore shakos except the Argentine Cadets whose headgear was a tall helmet with a white plume. Infantry of the Argentine had a blue-grey dress. The Uruguayan Military Cadets, slim young men, wore short blue tunics and white trousers and seemed to come out of the Peninsular War. The infantry had a khaki uniform. All carried rifles at the slope on the left shoulder and the butt was held over the chest in the French manner. . .

Over the course of the following years a number of other Argentine and Uruguayan boxes were put on the market, including a new issue of Argentine naval cadets, and the notorious steel-helmetted Argentinians of early 1939–40, part of the mélange of Germans, Poles, Dutch and Argentinians (Chapter 20). The Britains' directors and their artist, Fred Whisstock, loved to give these exotic sets titles in their native language. So we have flamboyant labels complemented by such names as *Los Alumnos de la Escuela Militar*, *Argentinos Granaderos a Caballo*, *Marina Argentina Cadetes Navales*, and so on. The hybrid shrapnel-proof Argentinians of the Second World War achieved respectability under the title of *Infanteria con Casco*. William Britain's sole trip into Mexican military history (Chapter 10) also had him indulging in the vernacular. His infantry of the time of Pancho Villa were labelled *Rurales de la Federacion* with the English words in parenthesis beneath, 'Mexico's Pride'.

Not until 1955 did the firm produce Venezuelans: military school cadets, infantry and sailors, bringing the total number of South and Central American sets in Britains' lifetime up to almost 20.

The Scandinavian commitment rests solely on three different figures, all produced after the Second World War. Britains' first Danish model was the *Garde Husar* Regiment in review order, issued with officer and trumpeter and based on the dashing Prussian Hussar of 1908: a short-lived and therefore today a rare figure. It was complemented by the *Livgarde*, a new foot figure in a feathered helmet. Soon they were to be joined by a Swedish soldier, the *Svea Livgarde*, in ceremonial dress, a reincarnation of the Argentine military cadets from across the other side of the world. Nothing was made of Norwegian soldiers.

In the Antipodes there was the Victorian diamond jubilee apparition of the non-existent 'South Australian Lancers' and then, much later, more accurate portrayals of the Australian and New Zealand armies. Their infantry, wearing respectively traditional headgear, came out both marching at the slope and standing to attention at the present in time to provide parade and street-lining fodder for displays based on the 1937 coronation of King George VI. A reign later, the Aussies were garbed in blue ceremonial dress to serve for any child who wanted to mount a coronation procession for Elizabeth II. Both Diggers and Kiwis have an affectionate spot in the hearts of today's collectors, their attractions being enhanced by the prices they bring, well up the scale of swop-and-buy values.

CHAPTER **23** CARRY ON, BRITAINS

What did Britains achieve in just over 70 years of lead soldiers? Malcolm Forbes, on the subject of toys, has written: 'The things of childhood have a lasting impression throughout one's life. If they are playwithable, imaginative and beautiful, it's important.' He was writing specifically about the *Forbes* Collection of toy boats*, but his words speak just as aptly for toy soldiers. They could stand equally well as an epitaph for Britains, were not the word 'epitaph' much too premature: though the veteran moulds gather dust in the vaults of its modern factory, the firm continues as a vibrant commercial proposition in a plastic and diecast toy world.

It can be justifiably argued that no other maker in the history of toy soldiers packaged so many different products in its lifetime (Dennis Britain's 'nightmare' of diversification), spread its net so wide across the world, or left such a rich field of choice for modern-day collectors.

Malcolm Forbes's nostalgia for his childhood toys is shared by thousands of collectors whose introduction to Britains was a shiny red box on a birthday or Christmas Eve. I remember, with some chagrin now, deciding that my modest boyhood collection was, in 1940, too thinly representative of the enemy, and applying field grey and green paint to a number of British infantry to turn them into Germans and Italians, thus regrettably destroying their collector value for posterity. At a younger age, the promise of a set of Britains' Black Watch for Christmas, this having been selected from the meagre stock of the local toyshop/newsagent, meant anxious daily visits to ensure that the proprietor, Mrs Mills, was keeping it for the big day, as my father, like any self respecting Lancashire man in cotton's depression, did not expect to pay until his Christmas savings clubs matured.

The magic of Britains was no less effective three thousand miles away across the Atlantic. A New York-based writer and editor, Henry I. Kurtz, has recently reminisced in print:

Toy Boats 1870–1955 A Pictorial History, by Jacques Milet and Robert Forbes. Charles Scribner's Sons, New York; Patrick Stephens, Cambridge, 1979.

I was a boy growing up in Brooklyn, back in the days when Ebbets Field was still home to the Dodgers. I collected toy soldiers. Not the dimestore variety, mind you, but the higher-quality lead soldiers with movable arms imported from Great Britain. I was 12 years old when I got my first set – eight stalwart Coldstream Guards in scarlet tunics and towering bearskin hats – at the Abraham and Strauss department store in Downtown Brooklyn for the grand sum of $1.69. In the years that followed, while the Dodgers added names such as Jackie Robinson, Duke Snider, and Gil Hodges to their roster, I added toy soldiers with colorful names – The Capetown Highlanders, The Duke of Connaught's Lancers, The Queen's Own Hussars – to the muster of my miniature army.

Times have changed. The Dodgers have long since departed Brooklyn and my old toy soldier collection has gone the way of most childhood playthings. And that's truly a pity, because if I still had those little lead troops, I could cash them in for a tidy sum. The same sets I paid $1.00 to $2.50 for 25 and 30 years ago now sell regularly at auction, and at speciality stores such as The Soldier Shop in New York City, for $75.00 and up. They have appreciated at the rate of 100 per cent or more a year, with prices skyrocketing since the mid-'70s.

Kurtz wrote this in 1979, and prices have moved up accordingly since then. He was following the pattern of most journalists when writing about Britains' lead soldiers – pondering on their remarkable record as an investment prospect. *Smithsonian* magazine, in its 1980 survey of toy soldiers and the *Forbes* Collection, had hardly got into its stride in an eight-page exposition before it was concluding that 'money there is in toy soldiers, ready and waiting . . . soldiers have come a long way since they were playthings for small boys and cost a carefully saved quarter or so apiece.'

Dennis Britain adopts an attitude of healthily amused tolerance to the meteoric rise in value of his old products. He sat, alone, in wonderment at the back of the Phillips auction room in the early boom days of the seventies, unrecognized by scores of Britains fanatics who were bidding the red-boxed sets up to record levels. 'If only I'd kept my toy soldiers,' is a common enough remark these days, as the high prices are publicized widely. Britain sees the irony and piquancy of it when he repeats the phrase, although he is far too philosophical to let his lack of foresight worry him. His compensation is the pleasure of seeing his family's life work being accepted as highly esteemed collectors' items and traded in leading international salerooms among works of art.

Some collectors pretend to eschew talk of prices and investment, arguing that true enthusiasts are being bid out of the market, but they cannot fail to acknowledge, if they are honest, that the steady price spiral for old Britains as witnessed in the auction rooms and specialist shops has measurably increased the value of their own collections, brought out into circulation hundreds of thousands of figures which otherwise would not have been available to collectors, and helped nourish the lore and bibliography of toy soldiers by stimulating the interest in collecting in most countries of the western world.

Their suspicions are understandable, however, on occasions such as in 1979 when an early version of a Britains' country curate achieved notoriety in the domain of Mammon by reaching the ridiculous price of £90 at auction, thus showing an appreciation performance of something over 100 000 per cent on its original purchase price in the twenties (beat that on the stock exchange, if you can!). Such a freak price merely means that two people in a particular saleroom on a particular day decided that they desperately wanted that particular parson, rare though he may be. Similarly, unprecedentedly expensive tunes were played by bands of the Salvation Army until publicity about the prices coaxed out more such bands from attics and closets; what was once the ultra-rare became, if not commonplace, a familiar feature of auctions and prices were muted accordingly.

Burtt Ehrlich, the president of a Wall Street securities firm, has, through the nature of his chosen vocation, an informed consciousness of the investment value of his carefully constructed and definitive collection of thousands of Britains which he displayed in thick ranks on a battery of shelves in his Manhattan apartment (his wife, Fran, has a wrily tolerant awareness of the collection's appreciation in *volume*!). But that apart, Ehrlich is unequivocal when he answers the question, '*Why* collect toy soldiers?' He says: 'Acquiring them is the fun. It's a very exciting game finding things before others do. I'm always looking for the great, hidden treasure. Can't resist it.' Like many collectors, he admits it's a bit of an addiction and when the Ehrlichs acquired a considerably larger apartment he cheerfully suggested the move was dictated by the logistics of his army.

The problem of expansion was no less acute for Remigio Gennari, architect, of Rome, whose many tens of thousands of troops – including a large and enviable contingent of Heydes – was quartered, in the words of his wife Livia, 'under beds, in closets, everywhere you look'. When he moved into and refurbished a new home in magnificent period premises in the heart of the capital in 1980, his professional eye not only supervised the domestic arrangements but saw that there were adequate parade facilities for his soldiers.

Although Gennari has a large library of military books and is, in particular, a specialist on the campaigns of Frederick the Great of Prussia, he is – like most collectors – a most unbellicose man. Steve Balkin, who knows as much about Britains' soldiers as anyone in New York and can be found at the Burlington Antique Toy Shop in Madison Avenue, says: 'Collectors are not a bunch of guys running around rattling their sabres. Very few of the people who come into my shop have more than a passing interest in battles and campaigns. It's the colour and the spectacle that attracts them – the troops on parade and the marching bands.'

Indeed, of the huge production of Britains from 1893 to 1967, comparatively few are in warlike poses, the majority being on parade. This has been the point of

Dennis Britain, retired chairman of the company, regards with tolerant amusement and amazement the prices now commanded by his lead armies. Here, he inspects a member of the Bikanir Camel Corps on viewing day at Phillips, the London auctioneers who pioneered regular sales of old lead soldiers.

criticism from some collectors who yearned for something of the frenetic activity of, say, Heyde of Germany, but part of the reason behind the preponderance of parade figures was commercial. William Britain and his successors never forgot that they were in the business to make money. They knew that boys preferred colourful uniforms to active service drab, so they put their troops in review order. And that meant marching, and playing bands, not fighting.

The Britains' dynasty can be proud of 'an achievement in British industry', as the foreword to the company's 1938 catalogue puts it. The philosophy behind this achievement is probably best summed up in the foreword's own text:

Every business has its individual history, whether it has climbed from small beginnings, gradually building up stone by stone, or whether it has blazzoned [sic] forth from obscurity in one single leap, and the business of manufacturing model Toy Soldiers and Model Home Farms has, perhaps, a history that is more individual than most.

The business was established in 1860 and in its early days the first Toy Soldiers were produced*, and since that time the Toy Soldier, whose prototype is perhaps one of the oldest things in history, has steadily gained favour with the youth of the world, until to-day there is probably no other toy which enjoys the same universal popularity.

This popularity is due as much as anything to the great care which Britains Limited have always taken to make their models true to life, and the amount of time and care spent on details in producing models has proved time well spent, as is evidenced by the ever increasing demands for them.

In conclusion, Britains Limited sincerely hope that a glance through the following pages will provide interest to those who already collect Britains Models by giving them particulars of models not yet in their collections, whilst to those who are not yet Collectors it will give some glimpse of the pleasures they have to come.

On every subsequent page of the catalogue the firm – aware that it was the subject of the greatest form of flattery, imitation – printed this piece of advice: 'WHEN BUYING BRITAINS SOLDIERS SEE THAT THEY ARE BRITAINS.'

---

*A slight case of blurb-writer's licence.

PART THREE

Anybody's Fight

Hitler by the German firm of Elastolin. He came in many poses, many uniforms, amid a gallery of Nazi leaders catalogued as *Führende Persönlichkeiten*. Today these personality figures command the highest prices, particularly at auctions in Germany.

There are two unsubstantiated stories that go the rounds among collectors of German composition figures; both concern the vanity of the Führer. One is that he 'leant' on the firm of Hausser, maker of Elastolin soldiers, to introduce porcelain heads for certain portrait figures of the hierarchy so justice could be done to facial features. The other is that a prototype figure of Hitler was not approved because it made him look too short. The stories may be true. Certainly porcelain-headed personalities began to appear in the Elastolin catalogue of 1936 – Göring was a notable recipient of a wickedly cherubic pot face – and German children were then and later offered a variety of Hitlers, ranging from a dais-ensconced automaton with a springloaded 'heiling' arm to a surprisingly seedy looking, cap-in-hand version in a brown raincoat.

Hausser, still in business in West Germany, discounts the argument that its production of toy soldiers and equipment, party organizations and offshoots, during the thirties and forties was manipulated by the Nazis and that the firm exploited the psychological climate of prewar and wartime Germany for commercial reasons. Kurt Hausser, son of a co-founder of the Elastolin empire, is on record as saying in recent years: 'We were a commercial company trying to do business during the sixty most cataclysmic years the world has ever known, the First World War, rampant inflation, economic depression, the Third Reich, the Second World War, postwar reconstruction. What a period, unlike no other in modern history.' Critics may detect a note of apologia, but support for his argument comes from Herbert Bechtold, an American and long-time collector of composition figures, who emigrated from Germany in 1935 to avoid conscription when 'its new army began to breathe down my neck' – and returned in 1944 as a soldier for Patton. 'The overall objectives of the German toy industry,' he says, 'were no different from those of counterparts in other countries – to be marketable and competitive with an attractive product, and to avoid the red ink on the bottom line of the balance sheet.'

Nevertheless, the emotive background of war toys in the Nazi era is such that questions, explanations and apologia abound when collectors go into print on this their specialized subject. The phrase, 'no inference should be drawn as to the political views of the author/contributor' is typical. Reggie Polaine, the British collector, felt impelled to make use of such a disclaimer when introducing the first fully illustrated English language work on Hausser-Elastolin in 1979. He highlighted the obvious pressures on the German makers when discussing Elastolin's enthusiastic commitment to models of Hitler's street thugs, the SA, and other uniformed party supporters with their blazing (battery-powered) torches and propagandist paraphernalia: 'There was no official encouragement of the manufacture of these politically based figures, but the political climate was such, that not to have produced them, would have quickly brought about official displeasure and on a commercial plane, a loss of sales.'

Hitler saw all too clearly the propaganda value of consumer interest in the battalions of starkly realistic figures goose-stepping from the factories of Elastolin and its competitors such as Lineol. At a period when, in the beleagured United Kingdom, the firm of William Britain was turning from make-believe to *real* war production for the second time in its history, the German toy soldier factories received official encouragement and material help as part of Hitler's policy to increase the production of goods for home consumption, a decision he came to because he believed the war was won after the fall of France in 1940. It was not until much later in the war that Elastolin had to make do – in the face of worsening shortages – with *ersatz* raw material, paint and labour, a situation which resulted in figures far below its traditional standards.

Emotions and recriminations apart, the pre-1945 era of Elastolin and Lineol has left collectors a rich field of pickings, of immense variety, and surprisingly large dimensions considering the ravages in Germany in the later stages of the war and the consequent destruction wrought under the de-Nazification and anti-militarism policy of the Allied Control Commission. Far from being simply a legacy of the Third Reich, the scope for collectors of composition soldiers covers a wide range of figures that represents a unique and brilliantly realistic contribution to the story of toy soldiers.

The Hausser brothers, Otto and Max, started making composition soldiers in 1904 in the town of Ludwigsberg, near Stuttgart in southern Germany, where they had been manufacturing and wholesaling dolls. The term Elastolin which they chose for their soldier products gives a clue to the plastic nature and ingredients of the material they used in a process similar to that employed in the making of dolls. With readily available cheap labour, equally available sawdust and glue was leavened with kaolin and linseed oil and the putty-like mixture was pressed into the two halves of a brass mould. Cheapness and simplicity were all. Into one part of the mould was placed a wire strengthener or basic skeleton. After the mould was closed it was lightly cooked in an oven, cooled, then opened and the resulting figure was finished and painted by hand. Lineol, subsequently Elastolin's principal rival, used a similar process but added rather more resin content in the mix; its composition closely resembled the currently commercial linoleum from which the firm borrowed part of its name.

Max Hausser was killed on the Western Front in 1915. Otto lived through his firm's international success and died in 1956, after seeing Elastolin rise from the ashes of the Second World War to a new, plastic future in Neustadt bei Coburg, which had become the company's home in 1936. His sons, Kurt and Rolfe, and Kurt's daughter, piloted Hausser into the post-war era.

Soldiers of sawdust and glue, the Elastolin *Wehrmacht* on parade: dramatically realistic despite their thick, heavy stands, but highly vulnerable to damp and excessive heat.

The figures of O. & M. Hausser, eventually rationalized into the 40- and 70-millimetre scale, present at first glance the appearance of carved wood. They are essentially German, as is their composition content. Lovers of Mignot, Britains or even German Heyde scorn the clumsy, thick bases and the even more clumsy wheeled wooden platforms on which the horses of gun and carriage teams stand. But the moulding techniques employed allow for some fine detail – down to a breast pocket button; and the huge range of imaginative activities and poses indulged in by Elastolin figures and groups more than makes up for their Teutonic grossness, which scale-wise makes them an incompatible mix with lead solids of other makers in Germany and elsewhere.

From the earliest days foot figures bore the name ELASTOLIN stamped under their bases in capital letters. From 1935 to 1936 the word GERMANY was added. Thereafter, the Elastolin part of the trademark appeared in cursive script. Otherwise, dating a figure can be a difficult task, relying much on catalogues which were issued up to 1940, and knowledge of social and military changes, as Hausser's records were destroyed along with its moulds during the war. So, too, were those of Lineol; but, worse in this case, the whole factory at Brandenburg, near Berlin, stock, moulds and even the firm's name were wiped off the face of the earth in the bombing. As one American Lineol buff puts it, 'Nobody cares to take the blame for hitting non-military targets, so we American collectors say it was the British.'

CHAPTER **25** **REALISM IN THE REICH**

Hausser plumbed Germany's history from Frederick the Great onwards and roved the military world in search of subject material in its first three decades, but often a foreign soldier – American, British, French, Italian – was given birth merely by cannibalizing an existing German torso. A quick lick of paint, khaki, blue, green, instead of field grey, sufficed over *Reichswehr* uniform; jackboots turned into puttees; a suitable plug-in head finished the job. Sticklers for accuracy among schoolboy customers in foreign countries were exasperated by the universal issue of the German 'potato masher' grenade to non-German assault troops, whether they were Doughboys, Tommies or *Poilus*. The answer was simply economic. To plug in a suitably helmeted head was easy. To provide the correct type of grenade meant a whole new body mould.

In addition to many other non-military figures and games, Elastolin did a strong line in zoo and Noah's ark animals, splendidly modelled and textured beasts that have still not reached their full investment potential among collectors, and in cowboys and Indians. The Wild West, always a source of curious fascination allied to glaring inaccuracy among German makers, found new expression in a multitude of camp-fire pastimes as well as the more obvious warring and hunting activities. Inevitably, however, the base 'collector power' of Elastolin lies in the huge mass of imaginatively designed and multi-varied figures, transport, armour, artillery and fortifications of the period through the thirties and leading into the war.

Present-day collectors who lived as children in Germany in the pre-Nazi period tell of a dearth of acceptable toy soldiers, especially in the early twenties in the areas under French occupation which fervently suppressed anything to do with German militarism. For the well-off child a few expensive Heydes were available in the shops, otherwise the choice was between crude and uninspired figures no better than the roughest of home castings, and remnants of flats or solids that had been handed down from earlier generations.

The cream of Elastolin production, geared for export, decorated showcases as rows of individual figures or red-boxed sets in stores like Macy's in New York, where one collector remembers in 1929 being dazzled by such a display laid out, symbolically, around the feet of an almost lifesize plaster Doughboy. (A few Elastolin and Lineol appeared now and again in certain London stores, but here the toy war machine of William Britain, revving up to its gigantic 1930s output, was unstoppable.)

In the south of Germany Elastolin flourished under a largely autonomous and right-of-centre regional government in more advantageous political and business circumstances than did Lineol in the Berlin area, with its socialist dominated regime. Manpower was expensive in the north, while Elastolin enjoyed the comparatively cheap labour of the cottage industries in the southern hills and mountains. Much of the trimming and painting was contracted out to home-workers. While socialist newspapers in Prussia railed at the pay and conditions of the 'exploited' toy soldier workers and campaigned for public boycotts, Hausser in the south basked in the glow of a paternalistic administration. The company, therefore, was much more strategically poised than Lineol to take advantage of the opportunities when Hitler's rise to power in 1933 created a new climate of nationalism, a temporary economic boom and a demand for better quality consumer goods for the home market.

The new *Wehrmacht, Luftwaffe* and *Kriegsmarine* provided immense scope for the toymakers. Their figures took on a more offensive, attacking posture, closer in spirit to the Third Reich's expansionist aims. Lineol, freed from its political trammels, took up the challenge with gusto and its new range of skilfully modelled figures, equipped with all the firepower and support equipment its designers could create, temporarily grabbed the lead from Elastolin. There followed an 'arms race' between the two principal makers that filled each issue of their catalogues with new figures in yet more exciting and animated poses, new vehicles that emulated the real thing so closely that sometimes the *Wehrmacht's* own security people had to step in to veto a detail still on the secret list, new ideas for static defences that made the traditional toy fort look like something out of the stone age. Elastolin, for example, marketed an add-on trench system that could be built up piece by piece into an elaborate front line, interlocking into sandbagged battery positions, radio outposts, field ambulance stations and underground bunkers. As the thirties moved to their ultimate destiny, the firm was ready with opposing Maginot and Siegfried line forts. In seven years its yearly production figures rose from half a million to three million (still notably less than the prodigious output from Britains).

Politics in prewar German was, to say the least, a tricky game. Even the toymakers knew that. Because of production schedules there was a large presence of SA models in Elastolin's 1936 catalogue, giving the impression that the brownshirted faction was in the ascendancy, whereas the reverse was the case. Next year, the aberration was corrected. When a name fell into disrepute, such as Roehm's in 1934, its Elastolin equivalent was not necessarily withdrawn as a portrait figure. It was either beheaded and given another identity or simply recatalogued as an anonymous senior officer. Goebbels surely approved of the pragmatism of it all.

Before the coming of Hitler, Hausser-Elastolin issued five portrait figures, Frederick the Great, two of his generals, Field Marshal Hindenburg and George Washington. When the Nazis arrived in power there was a whole rogues' galaxy of personalities, led by the Führer himself, from which to choose – *Führende Persönlichkeiten*, as the catalogue labelled the parade of power. Among them many a right arm is raised in salute. Today, arms are raised when these miniature reminders of the Nazi regime appear on the public scene, not in salute however, but to signify bids at auction where Elastolin and Lineol portrait figures command some of the highest individual prices in toy soldiery because of their rarity.

Choice of personalities was not always confined to Germans. Mussolini appeared in various mounted and dismounted poses, and with the accolade of a (somewhat large) porcelain head. Franco too is there. At the time of the Italian-Abyssinian war in 1935 Emperor Haile Selassie – together with a number of his colourful supporters and Italian opponents – stepped into the pages of Lineol's catalogue. The appearance of a non-Aryan among the portrait figures was, however, short-lived. By the time of his country's capitulation, the 1937–8 catalogue presented Haile Selassie with an overstamp, *Gestreicht* (Removed).

Although Elastolin and Lineol dominated the composition soldier scene in Europe, other firms prospered with figures usually of an inferior quality. Duro and Durolin were based in Czechoslovakia, Leyla in Nuremberg, Schusso in Austria. Armee was another independent. Italia made composition figures in Italy, Durso in Belgium and Danolin in Denmark. Like Elastolin and Lineol, most stamped their names beneath the bases of foot figures. Tipp & Co. (Tippco) produced tinplate guns and vehicles, the latter crewed by Elastolin figures made especially for the Nuremberg firm. (It was seized by the state in 1933 when its owner, Phillip Ullman, fled to Britain.) By arrangement Elastolin also manned the extremely realistic tinplate clockwork *panzers* of Gama and Gesha.

Under its family name of Hausser, the Elastolin firm made its own tinplate military vehicles in a range of accessories that stretched from field bakeries to massive tractor-drawn artillery. Its motorized field ambulance, which did a swift and cunning shift of identity as a radio command vehicle, came complete with opening doors, medical crew and realistically battered wounded. But pride of place was taken by a monster representing a war machine with the aptly formidable title of *Mittlerer Zugkraftwagen Sd Kraftfahrzeuge* – or mid-class towing diesel power motorized vehicle. This 14-inch halftrack with an 11-man crew and working headlamps seems to dwarf the rest of the Elastolin army. Its price in 1939 was commensurate, 30 marks, which was then a week's wage for many a German labourer.

The following year saw the last of the old-style Elastolin catalogues. Europe was deeply involved in a real war that was to spread across the world. Reason, like truth, tended as always to be an early casualty. Elastolin and Lineol displays vanished from the big stories in the United States: a New York newspaper of 1941 told of a German alien in Buffalo whose Lineol collection was seized by the FBI because it was considered subversive.

Elastolin survived the war and restarted production in the late forties. Lineol vanished; nothing has been heard of it from behind the East German curtain – though collector Herbert Bechtold tells a curious story about this name. His boyhood interest in Elastolin-Lineol was rekindled when he found a box of gun, caisson and soldiers under rubble in a German village house while serving in the US Third Army. Later, stationed in Berlin, he bartered candy and other food with townsfolk for their unwanted toy soldiers. then, in the late sixties, a fellow collector brought to him a figure of an East German army officer, crude and squat. Under the base was stamped the name, LINEOL. Does the East, he asks, guard a secret which the toy soldier world would like to crack?

CHAPTER **26** SOLDIERS OF SPAIN

In May 1978, my wife and I, as curators of the *Forbes* Museum of Military Miniatures, began unpacking a series of crates in the coolness of a newly built extension, where stood half a dozen glazed display cabinets, brand new, aggressively empty and awaiting the contents of those crates. As we uncovered layer after layer of lead soldiers by peeling off ancient tissue paper and rubbing away grime with moistened cloths, there came to us the echoes of what Hugh Thomas, the internationally known author, has described as 'a most passionate war' and a symbolic conflict, a clash between Christianity and atheism, reaction and liberal democracy, fascism and communism – the Spanish Civil War.

From under the grime, which was gunpowder black on many, there emerged the troops of that evocative era: blue-shirted Spanish Foreign Legionaries, their sleeves rolled up in characteristic style; *Requetes* of the Carlist regiments; *Guardia Civil* in their shiny black-patent leather hats; greycoated *Policia Armada*; the terrible *Regulares*, Franco's crack Moorish troops; line infantry and support units, in German style helmets. There were fleets of cyclists and motor cyclists, enough mules to populate every olive grove in Andalusia, and for about every ten combat men there were two medical orderlies, carrying long stretcher poles. Solid, full-round, quality varying from crude to excellent and size from 45 to 54 millimetres, the figures were at first glance akin to Heyde. Appendages such as arms, rifles and swords, which appeared hopelessly bent, proved very resilient and were easily straightened, so pliable was their metal. This was our introduction to Spanish toy soldiers.

They had been sold to the museum in Tangier as an entire collection of about 6000 by their Spanish owner, a resident of nearby Ceuta, the Spanish African enclave on the southern side of the Straits of Gibraltar. Part of the collection predated the Civil War; other parts were contributed by post-Second World War makers. Thus the task of identification produced the names of several leading Spanish firms – Casanellas, Palomeque, TEO, Sanquez, Martes and so on.

Little had been written about the development of Spanish toy soldiers until

Jose Manuel Allendesalazar, a most engaging diplomat in the American section of the Foreign Ministry in Madrid, produced a book in 1979 that cast much needed light on the subject (see bibliography). Subsequently, over lunch of duck *à la Sevillana* and an excellent bottle of Marqués de Murrieta at the Martinez Restaurant in London, the Spanish author and collector unravelled further mysteries surrounding these versatile, sometimes superior, and frequently underestimated figures. The story he had to tell is one closely enmeshed in the present century's turbulent history of Spain, to such a degree that the soldiers and the men who made them were often closely affected by the military and political movements they were portraying in miniature.

Spain's toy soldier industry which never enjoyed much sales success beyond the confines of the Pyrenees nevertheless owed its birth to foreign influence. The first tin flats were made in 1828 when Carlos Ortelli, an Italian from Como, set up in business in Barcelona, which was to become the principal centre of manufacture in Spain. Employing at first other Italian refugees as engravers, and producing 54-millimetre tin soldiers in the characteristic elongated style of early 'Nurembergs', he prospered in the amenable commercial environment of Catalonia. His flats were sold painted or unpainted, or as a variation, painted on one side only, and his lines included religious, dance, circus and seafaring subjects as well as military. A large number of his slate and metal moulds are preserved in the city's Pueblo Español museum where some are used today to produce tin soldiers as he did. Both Ortelli and Lleonart, another Barcelona tin soldier man, who flourished in the latter part of the century, faced tough competition in the shops from Heinrichsen and the soldiers of Mignot. There was some experimentation with semi-solids, but it was not until the first decade of the twentieth century that Barcelona produced its first commercial, full-round solids.

Leaders in the new field were Eulogio Gonzalez (remembered among collector circles by his first name) and Baldomero Casanellas. Eulogio, who lived until 1974 and the ripe age of 84, left a characteristic 'trademark' of a thin strip of metal which joined three hooves of his horses, thus dispensing with the need for a stand.

Bearing similarity to figures by Heyde of Germany, the Turkish gun team is by the Spanish maker Jose Capell, who flourished after the Spanish Civil War. All the men are detachable from their seats. The lancers in the foreground carry the colours of Italy on their pennants and represent Libyan native cavalry. Scale: 45mm.

Casanellas marketed his mainly 54-millimetre figures as *La Guerra* brand, and when he died in 1925 his business was carried on by his nephews, the brothers Capell. Both Eulogio and Casanellas benefited from the influence and patronage of a remarkable collector, Arturo Llovera, a naval man who had also served with the *Regulares* in Moroccan campaigns. Llovera provided them with documented and photographic research from which they made a 20 000-figure column representing an entire division on the march. Now owned by the Defence Ministry, the collection is housed in the Montjuich Museum in Barcelona.

From the 1920s to the outbreak of the Civil War in 1936, the Spanish toy soldier industry experienced many changes, the most outstanding being the emergence of the 45-millimetre solid as the dominant product. It was cheaper than the 54-millimetre and easier to marshal into large armies. Spain, too, was undergoing change and the political upheavals frequently had their effect on the manufacturers, just as they did on the rest of industry.

Teodoro Rodriquez, of Barcelona, whose allegiance to the 54-millimetre was firm, produced models of the highest quality that sported separate helmets and equipment such as cuirasses. His horses stood on their legs without base-stands. In 1931 he made a present to King Alfonso XIII of a superb squadron of the Royal Escort, arguably the best figures he ever made. But politics negated his gesture. Within a few weeks, a republic was proclaimed and by official decree the toys of the royal children were sequestered, including 'a group of very new soldiers of the Royal Escort'. Rodriguez's figures, sold under the name TEO, enjoyed little better success commercially. They were, undeniably, excellent, but they were too expensive – three pesetas apiece, compared with competitive figures at 30 centimos, foot, and 60 centimos, mounted. In 1932 he surrendered to the economic inevitable and soldiered on with products of an inferior quality.

Meanwhile, a contemporary, Pedro Palomeque, had broken Barcelona's virtual monopoly in 1922 by starting a lead soldier business in Madrid. It was to become Spain's best known and most successful toy soldier firm, with a large and much varied output considering it had a life of little more than 14 years.

Descended from the Toledo noble family of Villanueva de la Sagra, Palomeque first became a soldier then went into his father's business, a store selling religious items in the centre of Madrid. Then he set up a small toy soldier factory in a family house in the southern suburb of Leganes where, as we shall see, his employees exercised a remarkable initiative under a proprietorial *laisser faire* policy. Like Heyde, Palomeque and his workers believed in giving the public variety amid their sets of soldiers. Like Heyde, the business was to end in swift and terrible wartime violence.

In keeping with the uniquely unusual stamp of the firm, Palomeque employed as his principal engraver a Phillipino, described by Allendesalazar as 'somewhat Bohemian but gifted with patience and a skilful hand'. He paid him the then considerable sum of 500 pesetas a mould, and although there were never more than about 400 basic designs, the factory's figures appeared in a multitude of variations owing to the workers' versatility with soldering iron and paintbrush.

Apart from a fulltime staff of manager and two foundrymen, production lay in the hands of a number of local townswomen who earned four or five pesetas a day on piecework, finishing and painting. They seem to have been a delightfully inventive band who, with the owner's encouragement, excelled in giving figures individual touches. For example, Maria-Teresa might decide to give a rifleman a knapsack or forage bag, while next to her, Consuelo was adding the touch of a torn shirt to a cavalryman in action. From Dolores a grenadier might receive a bloodied bandage around his head or arm, while Asuncion would specialize in a nice line of decorated saddles for pack mules instead of the plain army issue.

It all helped to boost the sales of Palomeque's soldiers which were in demand at several big Madrid stores and sold in red, black or gold boxes according to quality.

Several months a year were spent in designing, making and assembling a huge diorama which was on shop window display in the Calle de Arenal in time for Madrid's principal spring *fiesta*. Exhibition gold medals enhanced Palomeque's reputation, and his figures gained in quality year by year. Then came the Civil War in 1936.

With his noble and military background, Palomeque was a known right-winger; almost immediately the Madrid Republican authorities detained him. He was released but took refuge in the Chilean embassy as fearsome retribution against Nationalist sympathizers became more widespread. Under a manager, production from the little factory – now almost in the frontline – came to a virtual standstill. Although the suburb of Leganes, a city tram terminal, was under constant shelling and bombing, the building escaped damage – until 5 November, when Franco's Army of Africa stormed into the town as a prelude to its offensive on Madrid.

By radio, Franco threatened: '. . . we shall know the guilty and only upon them will fall the weight of the law.' Desperately anxious to display the political affinities of the proprietor, Palomeque's manager placed a Nationalist flag in the doorway of the toy soldier factory. It didn't help. As Franco's fierce Moorish *Regulares* blasted their way along the Calle de Santa Rosa, they razed the factory to the ground. Behind them, the bronze soldier moulds were collected from the debris and turned into munitions with which to bombard besieged Madrid.

After seeking embassy shelter, Pedro Palomeque survived the three-year siege. But he never went back to making toy soldiers. Those of his figures that escaped the ravages of civil war are now prized collectors' items.

Spanish production suffered an inevitable slump during the Civil War, and was almost non-existent on the Republican side. Nationalist troops were represented among some poor quality semi-flats manufactured in the closing stages of the conflict, and it was not until the early forties that matters improved with some excellent 50-millimetre solids from the brothers Sanquez of Madrid. They had movable arms and were finely detailed down to uniform pleats. Martes, of Vallecas, produced some 45-millimetre soldiers, including a stately, greatcoated bagpipe and bugle band of the *Batallon de Ministerio de Ejercito* (Army Ministry), an example of which is in the *Forbes* Collection.

After that the palm goes to skilful and applauded firms such as Julio Alcocer and Jose Almirall, both of Barcelona, for their distinction in the field of military models rather than toys, and to Angel Comes, of Valencia, who has broken ground with a new size, 20 millimetres, in which he had produced a vast range of infantry of the world's armies under the name of Alymer.

No survey of Spanish figures is complete without a mention of the national spectacle, the bullfight, and most native manufacturers who covered non-military

Spanish in idiom but German in manufacture. The two figures are from a late nineteenth century bullfight group by Heinrichsen of Nuremberg, modelled in 30mm and reasonably accurate in its depiction of bull, matadors, banderilleros, picadors and attendants.

55 Contrast in styles between a twentieth-century field kitchen unit by the Spanish toy soldier maker, Garcia Castresana, and a field kitchen of the Napoleonic era by Mignot of France. Both groups employ the solid, full-round figure. Castresana flourished from the mid-forties to the mid-sixties.

56 Skiers by Castresana of Madrid, hooded, heavily coated and carrying slung rifles which can be detached, command an unusual but appealing team of dogs, each with its sled. Ski troops are rare; compare them with Britains' skiers on colour photograph 46.

Left

57 War by elephant: the enemy is a tiger. The British manufacturer, Timpo, produced this splendid group, with elephants that have often been converted by model soldier enthusiasts into armoured battle beasts.

58 War by elephant: the enemy is Rome. Hannibal's war elephant was produced in Japan, by Minnikin Figures, a firm noted for its remarkable product similarity to Heyde and Britains' wares. As Hannibal surmounted the Alps, so Minnikins have climbed over international trade barriers and penetrated soldier markets in the west in modern times.

59 Sick parade in the trenches – part of an entire 666-man strong battalion of the London Scottish Regiment in 1916, converted and repainted from Britains' figures. Students of Britains' civilians will recognize the medical officer conversion with pipe and coat on arm.

60 The mounted men and the front rank are Blenheim figures of both sides in the American War of Independence, created for the Princeton Battlefield Area Preservation Society. The three figures on the right are Nostalgia's veterans of the Indian Mutiny. All are examples of 'new old toy soldiers'.

61 These splendid characters are camel gunners of the 3rd Nizam of Hyderabad Cavalry, circa 1848, created by Nostalgia. The weapon they carried was a particularly powerful piece.

62 Far from the horrors of warfare, men of the Yorkshire Regiment decorate their Christmas tree, a toy soldier vignette from the imagination of Harold Pestana, a Maine geology professor who produced his own army, Soldiers of the Queen.

63 More of Pestana's Soldiers of the Queen – a wiring party at work. For his box label, Pestana borrowed a picture of Victoria from a bottle of Bombay Gin.

64 Malcolm S. Forbes, whose collecting zeal was responsible for the formation of the *Forbes* Museum of Military Miniatures, is painted here as balloonist and motor-cyclist by Claudio Bravo.

Right

65 And befitting the collection of a keen balloonist, this display – a Royal Engineers' observation section in the late nineteenth century – is a focal point of a large panorama of the British army in the museum. The balloon unit was a conversion by a collector, using large amounts of recasts.

66 The *Forbes* Palais Mendoub in Tangier, home of the world's most remarkable collection of toy and model soldiers. Behind the gleaming white walls, 70 000 veterans live in pampered retirement.

67 & 68 Atop the palace roof, a modern figure symbolizing Islam looks out across the Straits of Gibraltar to distant Spain . . . and a French Spahi of 1914 shares the same vantage point.

69 Palms, Bedouin, camelmen and whirling dancers fill a Moorish arch in the cool of the museum's interior.

70 Flats by Ochel and Heinrichsen, including Frederick the Great (*front centre*), go through rehearsal for their placing in a large diorama of the Battle of Leuthen which comprises 7000 figures and occupies a room of the *Forbes* Museum.

Right

71 A close-up of the central character in the Battle of Leuthen, Old Fritz, mounted on a grey by Aloys Ochel of Kiel, but adopting the pose given to him by Johann Gottfried Hilpert, 'father of the tin soldier'.

72 From the Battle of Leuthen, part of a multi-piece pioneers' unit engaged in roadwork and bridging on the Prussian side of the battlefield. The set, finely engraved and painted, is probably by Heinrichsen.

73 This scene shows how tin flats by several makers, including Heinrichsen and Ochel, can be made up into diorama display – in this case representing an imaginary battle of the Napoleonic wars. Here, Scottish Highlanders are about to be overwhelmed by charging French cuirassiers.

74 Thousands of flats by relatively modern German makers, including Neckel, make up a large museum display of the Western Desert campaigns of the last war. A riddle was posed by the black faced soldier sitting in the halftrack: was he meant to be a Libyan, or did he represent dreams of a German pan-African dominance? (see Chapter 35).

75 The artistry of Edward Surén of London is demonstrated in the following four close-ups of his creation, a diorama of the sixteenth century Battle of the Three Kings, in which Moroccan forces routed a European army. Here, the Moroccans smash into the Portuguese centre. In the middle distance, Don Sebastian's camp.

76 An overall view of the battlefield, showing the Portuguese supply train engulfed in the fighting. Priests and nuns are about to be overwhelmed.

77 Desperate defence by musketeers fails to stop the onrush of the Moroccan horsemen just before the rout. Portuguese artillery is abandoned.

78 Friend and foe are inextricably mixed as the red banners of Islam press forward. Three kings died that day, two in defeat, one before victory.

themes included *corridas* in their repertoire, either as flats, semi-solids or solids. One of the most attractive bullfight sets I have seen – tin flats – is in the *Forbes* Collection. It consists of 15 figures in stylishly acrobatic posture, representing a period prior to 1932 (when by law heavy mattress protection was introduced for the picadors' horses). It is not, however, home produced. The label on the original box reads *Stiergefecht* and reveals the source as Heinrichsen, yet another example of Germany's tin figure hegemony.

CHAPTER **27** HOMEFRONT OPPOSITION

'There was never any doubt in our minds that our biggest competitor wasn't German, wasn't French. No, the most formidable rival to Britains was right here, in London – John Hill and Company.' Dennis Britain's view is delivered without a second's hesitation, the former head of the world's most successful toy soldier firm adding somewhat ruefully, 'They took two good casters from us.'

The last remark is something of an understatement, for it was a former Britains' employee named Wood who started Johillco – as most collectors know it – in 1900 before Dennis Britain was born. It was one of eight soldier companies, mostly producing 54-millimetre hollow-casts in the Britains' tradition, which began in London between 1900 and 1914. Some, like Renvoize, Reka and Hanks Brothers, are remembered today largely for their publicity-attracting attempts at piracy. By the end of the First World War only Johillco and Reka (off the scene by 1930) remained to resume business.

It is the opinion of Shamus Wade, the British collector, and originator of Nostalgia models, that Johillco 'produced some of the finest and some of the worst toy soldiers ever made' (*Old Toy Soldier Newsletter*). Most collectors would agree with him. Among the 'bads' he lists the all too common charging figure of the flat capped British Tommy; the 'goods' include Johillco's Mountie. Many would also agree with his further reasoning on this subject:

The 'soul-lessness' of so many Britains figures is perhaps due to an historical accident. When Britains first brought out their movable arm figures, this was a great innovation. It became a big selling point and they stuck to it most of the time. However, it did have one big disadvantage – there is not much you can do with a movable arm infantryman except make him march at the slope or trail. Johillco did not bother much about movable arms and so were able to give their figures a greater variety of poses. Another factor was that most Britains figures were sold in boxes of 5 or 8, while the majority of Johillco models were sold singly.

The same argument is also true about the once collector-despised American dimestore figures, and is developed in chapter 29. Here, a socio-economic point arises. Just as the dimestore figure in the United States appealed to the lower end of the schoolboy market in contrast to the more expensive imported wares, so Johillco soldiers tended to be price-competitive against the rather more snooty Britains. How many remember the agonies of decision in trying to decide whether to spend a modest boyhood windfall on a boxed set of eight Britains infantrymen or to buy maybe twice the number of individual Johillco figures? At the self-admitted risk of being abstruse, Wade takes it a little further: 'I have found that Johillco figures turn up more often in working class than in upper class households. . . . And it does not appear to have been just a question of money. Could it be because Johillco Other Ranks are individuals ("Look, it's just like

Uncle Charlie"), while Britains Other Ranks are obedient, anonymous and identical figures ordered about (in step) at the behest of their betters?'

Whatever the answer, Johillco, in the shadow of Britain's glories, ran a successful business, with huge exports abroad, mainly to the United States, in the inter-war years. Their foot soldiers were infinitely better than their horsemen, their strength lay in the British army rather than foreign armies. But there were many excellent foreign troops, notably their series of Abyssinians for the 1935 war – tribesmen, infantry, medics and mountain mule battery, the last being a gem of a collectors' item. The firm was responsible for the occasional aberration of scale that would have incensed a Britains' devotee: an 18-piece set included three bomber planes and a tank that were hopelessly out of scale with the accompanying soldiers and airmen. But their figures (usually marked with the company name or JOHILLCO) compared well with Britains and can often be mistaken for them at first glance, not only the military but civilian lines such as farms, zoos and rail personnel. And, like Britains, Hill did not forget the girls, producing (in defiance of any thirties women's lib) a range of household utensils specifically for that market.

The firm never again achieved the peak of production which it enjoyed just prior to the Second World War. Its factory at Tottenham was destroyed in the London blitz, and after the war it reopened at Burnley in Lancashire. In 1960 it went into liquidation, just before lead toy soldiers generally were phased out.

By this time a new batch of competitors to Britains had come into existence. The inter-war years had seen claims, of varying lifespans, from Charbens, Crescent, and Taylor and Barrett. After the war, Cherilea Products and Fylde and Company opened in Blackpool, and merged in 1950. Another, Timpo (Model Toys by 1953), was to be the most successful post-war newcomer, carving into Britains' home and export business in effective fashion. It produced some of the finest Second World War GIS ever made by a toy firm and had resounding success with a series of 'age of chivalry' figures based on the subjects of Hollywood films, Ivanhoe, Knights of the Round Table, and Quentin Durward. The heirs of Timpo have lasted in the toy business to present times.

A brief but fruitful appearance was made around 1950 by Selwyn Miniatures, an enterprise which flourished in a workshop over a London garage, fuelled by the genius of a brilliant designer, Roy Selwyn-Smith, and the capital of Otto Gottstein, the refugee from Nazi Germany. Smith had come out of the merchant navy, where he was a radio operator aboard fishing trawlers, to start a new career in the toy business of M. Zang, a Pole. There, he remembers making some strange composition toy soldiers. 'Metal was still very scarce,' he recalls, 'and we used to make a mix of pumice powder and glue. You mixed it hot, like a big dough, then pressed it into the mould. You then put the mould on a block of ice until you could remove the figure, now like a piece of stiffer dough. It was then placed on racks to finish off the drying process.'

Gottstein, impressed by Smith's design capabilities, helped set him up in his own business. It lasted only seven months and ended with Gottstein's death, when the firm's effects were sold. Smith went back to Zang and developed plastics. But a meeting with Joe Thake of Britains (who became chairman in December 1978) at Brighton Toy Fair led to a new job. Britains also bought up Zang's Herald series of toy soldiers, and Smith took a leading part in master-minding its development. A superb set of Smith creations was re-issued as Knights of Agincourt. Full-round, lead toy soldiers had never been as dramatically animated as these figures, which compared in quality of design with the connoisseur models of Richard Courtenay. Since then Smith has played a key role in Britains' build-up into a major international toy company in a diecast and plastic world.

No story of toy soldiers is as international as that of Comet (of Queens, New York) and its offshoots. Founded in 1919 as a diecasting business by Abraham

Authenticast, American based and wildly international in ramifications, is represented in this American Civil War line-up by the two figures on the extreme right, of undistinguished finish but possessing lifelike animation. They were made in the Irish factory. Next to them are two Heydes. The rest are Britains.

Slonim, Comet Metal Products was by the late thirties producing an undistinguished line of 55-millimetre solids. By this time, Abraham's sons, Joseph and Samuel, were in the company. Whereas the United States' involvement in war ended or interrupted the lives of many toy firms, it was the making of Comet. The firm switched to the production of military recognition models for use by the Services.

As the *New York Times* put it in an article on Comet on 13 September 1959, 'Three days after Pearl Harbor, Comet was in the scale model business in a big way.' The first of 10 million identification models were 50 000 warships ordered by the US Navy. In 1977 when the Douglas Fairbanks Junior collection came to auction in London, some of these ship models – together with others made by H.A. Framberg of Chicago – were among the lots. I bought a small fleet which included not only American and British warships such as the New Mexico, Saratoga, Hood and Warspite, but the French battleship Richelieu, and Germans like the Bismarck and Scharnhorst. At that time Douglas Fairbanks Junior told me that, whereas the Britains soldiers had been partly his boyhood playthings, partly a collector's indulgence, the ships had been for real: as a serving naval officer in the war he had used them in learning to identify friend and foe – 'And very good they were, too . . . being three-dimensional, they taught you the look of a vessel from all angles, including aerial.'

During the war Comet ran every hour of every day, seven days a week, 'while armed men patrolled the grounds guarding the ''classified work'' inside the ivy-laced brick building. Certainly the light irony of soldiers guarding a soldier factory must not have been lost on the workers'.★

After the war, the now prosperous Comet developed its international links. First, the Swedish Connection. A Swedish military attaché in the United States, Curt Wennberg, with experience in toy soldier production, had advised the firm on designs. Probably through him, Comet contacted Holger Eriksson, a designer in Sweden, who began to supply the creative power for a new and highly successful

★'Comet's Authenticast', by Steve Sommers, with Stacy Holmes and George Keester, *Old Toy Soldier Newsletter*, June 1979.

series of toy soldiers known as Authenticast. Next came the Irish Connection. With eyes on the market in Europe, Comet split its production between New York and the Republic of Ireland, where a factory was opened at Cladagh, Galway, taking advantage of Irish government aid to encourage industry in under-developed areas.

About 1947 Stacy Holmes, the Boston collector, remembers visiting the Richmond Hill, Long Island, plant of Comet. 'Castings were being made in the Long Island factory,' he says. 'These were then shipped to Eire for painting and returned to the USA for package and distribution. Later, casting as well as painting was done in Eire. They were well travelled troops by the time they reached the ultimate purchasers.'

The English Connection developed through a former prewar business associate of the Swede, Wennberg, who was now in charge of production in Galway. This associate, Fred Winkler, had established by the late forties a toy workshop in Deal, Kent. The business became Authenticast's main hope of conquering the English toy soldier market. It didn't quite work out that way. Production difficulties in Ireland affected the supply of Authenticast soldiers, and disaster eventually struck in 1950 when fire destroyed the Galway factory. Comet continued to produce figures in the United States, but without any authorized connection with the master designer, Holger Eriksson.

Meanwhile, Wennberg, burned out of a job, was establishing the South African Connection. He moved to Capetown with Eriksson's permission to use his designs in a range of figures for a new company, Swedish South African Engineers, SAE. Painting was done by African labour, surely a 'first' in toy soldier history. But the figures were a disappointment, unworthy of Eriksson's designs. SAE drifted on towards the end of the decade, and in New York Comet's lead soldier output was gradually reduced. Today, the products of this convoluted business exercise often appear in quantities at auctions, presenting collectors with a fascinating, if sometimes frustrating, task of identification.

A footnote to the Comet story and an interesting sidelight on international marketing and pricing problems has been provided by Stacy Holmes, who has made available correspondence with an English supplier when Holmes was acting as assistant to the general manager of Filene's, the Boston department store, after his return from the US Navy in the Pacific. Holmes was answering a query about the availability of American-made quality lead soldiers covering American historical periods. On 11 November 1947, he wrote:

At the present time there are only two active manufacturers of metal figures in this country that I know of, the principal one being Comet Metal Products Company in Long Island who have their original models made in Sweden, make the moulds here in this country, ship the moulds to Ireland for casting and painting, and then the finished figures are shipped back to this country for sale. They correspond somewhat to W. Britain's figures. Although they are solid castings, the actual sculpture is very good, but the painting is terrible.

These figures retail for about $2.00 for a box of seven, and they cover the periods that I think would be the most interesting and most saleable should you start [making] American figures; namely, the Revolutionary War with Minutemen, British Redcoats, and Rangers, such as the Virginia backwoodsmen. The next most popular figures would probably be such colorful historic personages as Buffalo Bill, General Robert E. Lee, General Custer and his troopers, Sitting Bull, and Indians of the famous 'Custer's Last Stand' fight.

I truly believe that your own Medieval figures have fully as much glamour in the eyes of American collectors and that there is no particular reason for you to risk the increased expense of new moulds for American figures, much as I would enjoy seeing them.

The person he was addressing was Britains' Richard Courtenay who, with his wife, had already achieved international repute for a splendid series of historical *model*, rather than toy, figures. They were mainly foot and mounted English and

French knights of the fourteenth century, resplendent in armour and colourful heraldry. Stacy Holmes first came across Courtenay knights in the Burlington Arcade, London, in 1936, and subsequently amassed a collection of them which he built into a diorama at his home in Chestnut Hill, Massachusetts. Therefore, he had a personal interest in the decision of Filene's parent group, the Associated Merchandising Corporation (including Bloomingdale's in New York, Hudson's in Detroit and Bullock's in Los Angeles) to buy Courtenay's entire output for distribution in the United States. This was, of course, at the time when metal was allowed for British soldier manufacture only if it was for exports.

Courtenay had his doubts about the type of figure he was supplying and the prices he was asking. 'I never feel quite certain that the periods I cover are the ones which most interest the American collector,' he had written from Slough in Buckinghamshire, in the enquiring letter which had produced the sound advice from Holmes, the marketing man: stick to what you do best.

As to prices, Courtenay's less expensive foot figures then retained in Boston at $4.50 each, the elaborate mounted pieces at $15 each. 'But,' says Stacy Holmes today, 'bear in mind that the dollar was worth about four times as much in 1947 as it is today. Thus a mounted knight would be at the equivalent of $60 in current dollars (sob!).' His response to Courtenay was that nothing but a radical reduction would make the sales any faster because people who collected Courtenays in the United States were 'those who really appreciate exquisite craftsmanship and to whom price is no particular barrier.' Courtenay took the advice: he hardly had any option, for, as he pointed out in a subsequent letter to Boston, 'Prices for everything have gone up tremendously. Example – metal prewar £20 a ton, now over £100 a ton. . . .'

Some 33 years later, in October 1980 – almost to the day that the modelmaker opened his correspondence with Stacy Holmes – a large cast of Courtenay knights took their cue on the stage of a former vaudeville theatre at 525 East 72nd Street, Manhattan. This is one of the New York salerooms of Phillips, the international fine art auctioneers, and it was one of their specialized sales of toy and model soldiers. After the sale I was able to give the news to Peter Greenhill, who with his wife, Gillian, produces Courtenays in the traditional style, after acquiring the moulds from Hummels, of Burlington Arcade, London, in 1978, 15 years after Richard Courtenay's death.

Roy Selwyn-Smith, whose medieval knights of Agincourt are among the most excitingly 'alive' full-round toy soldiers ever made, works on a Wild West scene. After leaving the sea, his career took him into toy soldier design and the managing director's chair at Britains.

At auction the competition for the veterans of the 100 Years' War was fierce – between dealers, private collectors and those attracted to the colourfully accoutred knights because of their brilliant investment potential as minor works of art. The prices broke many records, reaching as much as $500 a piece. Once again, the Black Prince, Lord de la Warr and Sieur de Chateaubriand were making history.

CHAPTER **28** PERSEVERANCE JONES

In a long, rambling and often turgid booklet that served both as an advertisement for his toy soldier firm and as a kite-flyer for a book he hoped to publish, one J. Edward Jones of Chicago, quoted in 1948 the advice of a contemporary military miniaturist on the subject of making one's own dioramas: 'Let simplicity be your watchword, effect your objective; let the lordly expert, with his head full of technical hairs just waiting to be split or started, according to the circumstances and spelling ability, control his superiority and restrain his tortuous ambition.'

If the words were sonorous – and they were certainly in keeping with J. Edward Jones's own lofty style – the sense was sound. Unfortunately, as toy soldier history knows, Jones was incapable of heeding the wisdom of the advice. If, in a long career of soldier-making, any man consistently practised splitting technical hairs and starting commercial hares, it was J. Edward Jones of Chicago, arguably one of the worst businessmen who ever poured lead into a mould hoping to make an honest buck out of it. Most of the stories of lead soldier manufacturers here being told record success in varying measure. J. Edward Jones's is the story of the great American failure.

Heaven knows, it was not for want of trying: he doggedly persevered from the mid-1920s right through to the mid-fifties, leaving us today with a fascinating legacy of one man's attempt to wrest supremacy from foreign competition for the American lead soldier. In the end, it was that foreign competition, allied to his own lack of business acumen, which beat him. Slapped sideways, financially floored, he came back fighting time after time when less resilient men would have thrown in the towel. The trouble was that Jones didn't know when to give up. Moreover, he desperately lacked selectivity and discrimination. His 1948 booklet is evidence of this. Its title page bears a bewildering multiplicity of titles:

LOOKING for a good hobby?
MINIATURES
provide the answer
Many sided as a diamond
Fun for young and old
An alluring
and enduring
hobby for all!
Read interesting
details herein

. . . and those were just *some* of his headings.

Seldom, if ever, has a toy soldier man in the course of his manufacturing life produced his wares under as many names as did Jones. Don Pielin and Steve Sommers have collaborated in *Old Toy Soldier Newsletter* in charting some of this remarkable man's career, which was marked by 'false starts, unfulfilled hopes, comic-tragic incidents, and apocryphal tales'. They suggest he may have started making 54-millimetre figures about 1925 with the laudable plan of producing a representative figure from each American war. With typical Jonesian timing, he chose the year 1929 to launch his first formal company, Metal Art Miniatures, and he commissioned moulds from a firm in Birmingham, England. The depression put paid to the venture, however, and by April 1931, Metal Art was dead. Undeterred, Jones within a few months returned to the arena as Miniature Products Company on South Michigan Avenue, Chicago. The British company, saddled with the moulds he had ordered, was glad to sell them to him at bargain rates of £9, or $31, for foot soldiers, £13, or $44, for cavalry; a point scored to J. Edward Jones. But by 1936 Miniature Products had gone the way of his first company.

In the meantime, there had been incidental ups and downs in the Jones story. A notable down occurred on a Chicago suburban bus ride in the early thirties. What is regarded as his first *hollow*-cast figure, a soldier of Wayne's Legion, was made for the 1933 Century of Progress event in Chicago. The mould, marked auspiciously No. 1, was lost when Jones left it on the seat of a city bus when hurrying off at his stop. Bad luck and his own failings haunted him. Acquaintances say he was dogged by his inability to fill orders, a tendency to advertise lines never actually in production, problems with creditors, and difficulties in getting his figures painted by home help in the volatile Chicago labour market of the thirties.

By 1940, he had teamed up with a partner, Ella Louise Hume, who provided the money for yet a new company, Metal Miniatures. It, too, collapsed, this time because of wartime shortages of metal. Jones joined the navy. Came 1946 and he was back in business again in the Windy City, with what was to become his best known firm, Moulded Miniatures.

Under the headline, 'Capture America's stirring past,' the somewhat confusing first entry in his list of wares was English bowmen and knights of the Third Crusade, followed by French infantry of the War of the Austrian Succession. He did, however, also offer Indians and British soldiers in the North American campaigns of the Seven Years' War, opposing sides of the American Revolution, those of the war of 1812, Civil War combatants, and denizens of the Wild West. His list came right up to date with a wide range of Second World War soldiers. His leaflet promised: 'This is only a brief listing of some of our production. New items created frequently.' Indeed, they were.

Therein, perhaps, lies the reason for Jones's difficulties. His products were too diversified. (Britains, of course, could also be accused of over-diversification – Dennis Britain's 'nightmare' of production lines – but here was a company based on sound traditions and with carefully tested markets, which never lost sight of its

American dimestore toy soldiers were crudely modelled in comparison to many European imports, but they had a verve and variety that endeared them to generations of boys in the United States. Above all, they were cheap. These motorcyclists are by Barclay.

true commercial aims.) Jones certainly thought big, when thinking miniature. His figures came in 54-millimetre (or 2¼-inch), 3-inch and 6-inch size. and included alongside his quality models some dimestore contributions. He seemed to have little control over methods and styles of painting; therefore his soldiers have no standard appearance to help identification today. When he sold his moulds during hard times, other people made soldiers from them, thus confusing the issue even further. His own castings varied from fragile shells to almost solid models. The names of his trade marks in post-war years varied as alarmingly – Moulded Miniatures, Varifix, Universal, Loyart and a second-generation Metal Art.

Soldiers were not the entire horizon of Jones. He ran a nebulous organization called the Visual History Association which published intermittent issues of a journal in the mid to late forties, and he planned one day to bring out a definitive tome on the hobby of miniatures. He died in 1957. No one could accuse him of lack of perseverance in his ambition to be a great toy soldier maker. Circumstances, it seemed, conspired against him.

Paul A. Lyon, a collector of Findlay, Ohio, has provided evidence of Jones's doubts and misgivings – particularly about foreign competition – in a letter the Chicagoan wrote to a Boston collector, the physician Howard K. Thompson, in September 1948. Referring to his wordy booklet, Jones wrote: 'This is merely an abridgement of a much larger manuscript which I hope to print in 1949 if business is any better – it couldn't be much worse due to British imports having upper hand.' He enclosed a list of some ambitious new lines he was planning for the following year, '*IF* business improves.' There was a truly Jonesian flavour about the postscript: 'Excuse the pencil. Typewriter has a key broken today.' It was just another setback on the commercial road of J. Edward Jones.

The redoubtable Perseverance Jones was not alone in his eccentricity, a quality as prevalent in toy soldier making as in any other industry. There was S. Chichester Lloyd, of the Saint Louis Lead Soldier Company, unabashed pirate of other people's designs, master of hyperbole, who flourished from about the mid-twenties. His Romans and knights were 'simply beyond description,' trumpeted his catalogue. 'Brilliant, sparkling, gorgeous, scintillating colors that appeal to you like a symphony.' Whether or not they lived up to the description, they were about the best out of a production that ranged from weird monstrosities such as seven-inch long mounted figures, to downright abysmal copies and remoulds of Britains, Heyde and Haffner. His piracy often led to cavalier, and sometimes hilarious, disregard of frontiers: John Garratt has unmasked Lloyd's George Washington as a kidnapped Frederick the Great, and General Foch of France hiding in a German Death's Head Hussar uniform.

CHAPTER **29** POD FOOT AND FRIENDS

In the fifties, about the time the world was shuddering at the depredations of *The Beast from 20000 Fathoms* and nightmares were being stage-managed by The Thing, Them, and It, after evenings at the local picture palace, there was on the scene a creature who – even if he was of benign intent and nursed no ambitions of cinematic infamy – bore a name menacing enough to join the cast of horrors then currently being dredged by Hollywood from the primeval slime and sub-conscious gloom.

Pod Foot.

He came in the wake of Short Stride and Long Stride, two more names that might have hopped or loped from the *dramatis personae* of those fantasy genre movies. No monster in size, Pod Foot grew – like Short and Long Stride before him – to little more than three inches in height. But he and the others came in millions, flooding the United States, swarming through stores, invading homes. What a scenario Hollywood missed!

Several generations of Americans have had affectionate regard for Pod Foot and his antecedents. They were dimestore soldiers all, given their strange descriptions according to their manner of stance. More specifically, the three came from the Barclay Manufacturing Company, named after a street in its birthplace of West Hoboken, New Jersey, and although the biggest of the American toy soldier makers in the inter-war years, just one of many that existed to supply dimestore America with cheap, easily produced lead figures. To a collector, Short Stride denotes the stiff-legged model of the early thirties in Barclay's young days; Long Stride came later in the same decade; Pod Foot, no longer reliant on a square or oblong base, plodded on to the scene in the decade immediately after the Second World War, with feet exactly as his name suggests.

That the study of dimestore soldiers should rely on such basic anatomical terms of identification, in the absence of a catalogue terminology founded on named and known regiments, is in itself an admission that this field of collecting lacks the rich vein of accuracy and attention to detail that attracts, say, the Britains, or the Mignot, or the Elastolin/Lineol enthusiast to his particular area of military miniatures. This is a personal view, and the voicing of it risks the wrath of the dimestore followers in the United States who, rightly take very seriously their study of the country's toy soldier heritage; their support of the cause, involving painstaking dedication to search and documentation of a large and diffuse industry has progressively changed the attitudes of other collectors in the space of only a few years from amused contempt, to benevolent tolerance, and finally to admiration.

It would still require mountains to move a Britains' man from his own loyalties into the dimestore camp. He could justifiably argue that there was little interest for him in a genre of soldiers in which rarely – very rarely – specific regiments are depicted or identifiable. His equivalent of the Pod Foot syndrome would be the terminology used to describe certain stages in Britains' manufacturing development, such as the cavalry on 'one-eared' horses, the lancer's mount with 'twisted rear legs', and the 'pigeon-chested' infantry. But these and other similar terms usually specified early Britains' anatomical aberrations which were in time corrected; and from the beginning, the figures which incorporated them fairly faithfully represented designated units, exemplified by the Life Guards, 5th (Royal Irish) Lancers, York and Lancaster Regiment and others . . . and so on into a list of many hundreds of famous regimental names.

The dimestore soldier usually, but not invariably, came as the home-bred Doughboy or GI, sailor or airman. Generically, he was an American fighting man. Essentially, he was made to be sold individually. Therefore, as a glance at Barclay's retrospective collectors' roll-call will show, he appeared doing a huge variety of interesting things (many more than Britains, incidentally), but was seldom dignified as the member of a named unit or corps: advancing with levelled rifle; kneeling with pigeons; walking with boxes; looking through rangefinder; wounded, sitting, arm in sling; cameraman, kneeling; doctor with stethoscope; cook holding roast; soldier peeling potatoes; wounded on crutches; falling with rifle; crouching with binoculars; typing at wooden table. . . . You could buy a hundred soldiers, doing a hundred different things, whereas the Britains traditional system of dispensing soldiers in infantry sets of eight and cavalry sets of five tended to limit the variety of modestly financed collections on economic grounds alone (although some Britains, including the cheaper ranges, could be

Barclay's Pod Foot soldiers plodded on to the dimestore scene after the Second World War, so named because of their distinctive stance. They usually represented American fighting men, as in this line-up of grenade thrower, bazooka operator and Marine.

bought individually). If it was make-believe and sheer, frenetic action-for-money that you wanted, the dimestore legions provided it in abundance – in much the same way that Germany's Heyde soared to much higher flights of imagination than the much more accurate, but pedestrian and parade-ground oriented Britains and Mignots.

The dimestore soldier *was* a different animal. He was crude but charming, endowed with endless variety, vitality and energy, and above all – cheap. He owes his very existence, ironically, to the invading competition of the United Kingdom, Germany and France. The lucrative target of high-quality soldier imports for most of the lifespan of the lead toy soldier during this century, the United States (and to a similar degree Canada) never really raised its own corresponding industry off the ground. Time after time, when delving into correspondence of American soldier manufacturers in the preparation of this book, research has uncovered the misgivings and the fears of American-based producers about the dominance of quality foreign imports.

By the time toy soldier entrepreneurs on the East Coast got around to thinking about capitalizing on what was a market of great potential – in the late twenties and early thirties – Britains, followed by Heyde, Mignot, Elastolin and Lineol were already firmly entrenched in the front line of the big stores, from Macy's in New York, to Marshall Field in Chicago, and right across the continent to the West Coast. There had to be an answer, and it was found at the very bottom of the market, in a soldier that could be made and sold more economically than the foreigners. That the dimestore warrior was to become the all-American fighting man was more than just patriotism and coincidence. It was commercial expedience.

Cheapness demanded a range of merchandise that was free of production line hiccups of the type caused by re-tooling for substitute heads when a national helmet had to be depicted. It allowed for no complicated paint charts and expensive changes of paint (Britains' record of ten paint changes on a single figure was out of the question!). Dimestore home-based painters were notoriously undisciplined by rules and regulations from the parent factory, which in many cases was a small shop with a handful of staff and under the control of a proprietor whose desire for quick bulk sales far outstripped his desire for accuracy or even knowledge of military sartorial matters. Therefore 'crazy' painting is well known and affectionately regarded by collectors of the dimestore variety: combat troops in white and green, silver and grey, silver and khaki were, for example, just a few of the apparitions from Manoil, a prolific, New York-based firm.

Manoil's experience in marketing was evidence of another factor that motivated against carefully planned catalogue series of regimental groups. Distribution throughout the United States was uneven. It depended on deals with individual stores. Often, if a big store or chain liked a particular model – i.e. if it sold well – the pilot issue was put into major production. If not, it was scrapped. Such a system has made for an interesting situation, from a collector's point of view, in which unsuccessful figures which had a short commercial life have a value far above the money-spinners of the day, but it did not encourage the better, more-organized manufacturers to embark on planned programmes of issues, regiment by regiment, country by country, as Britains did.

Isolationism in the United States in the thirties – a time when European toy soldier makers were mostly at the peak of their excellence – must also have affected the nature of the dimestore output. The American boy with limited pocket money to spend was regrettably poorly served when it came to foreign troops. European soldier makers had long been steeped in the, commercially sound, tradition of issuing troops of each side when a war broke out. But Manchuria and Montenegro were a long way from Minneapolis in 1904 and 1914, and distant wars were still only faint echoes in the Middle West in the thirties.

CHAPTER **30** DIMESTORE EMPIRES

The approach of the Second World War broadened the horizons of the dimestore soldier, but there had already been some earlier breaches of his all-American armour. In the mid-thirties when the world focus switched to the Far East, Barclay, among others, took note. From the New Jersey company came a familiar mounted figure but painted with variously coloured jacket and believed to represent Chinese or Japanese. About the same time, there is record, some Barclays were produced of a man bearing the Cuban flag, but these were a specific order for Woolworth's in Cuba.

An event that seems to have touched the United States with the same shocked effect that it had in Europe was the invasion in 1935 of Abyssinia, or Ethiopia, by Mussolini's Italian troops. It was reflected in dimestore, as it was in European, toy soldiers, even if in the former instance it was often a case of putting brown Ethiopian faces on some existing models and green Italian uniforms on others. Several Barclay figures of this war have been recorded by Richard O'Brien, specialist writer on old toys, comic strip creator, press agent and dimestore enthusiast. With the characteristic attention to detail inherent in his retrospective cataloguing of dimestore soldiers (*Collecting Toys*, 2nd edition, Books Americana, 1980) he lists one of these vintage models as 'Italian Infantryman, circa 1935–36, all known examples seem to have rifle tip broken off. Not known if there was a rifle tip.' (In 1980 he estimated the value at Good $6, Very Good $9, Mint $12.) Anybody know of an Italian invader with a rifle tip?

The Ethiopians from Barclay were robed tribesmen, therefore the product of a fresh mould and not merely repaints. A new figure, too, was their officer, but he was dressed in more conventional western (or eastern) uniform of tunic and trousers and thus became a ready candidate for re-issue a couple of years later as a

Japanese officer in new colours, notably yellowish face. Grey Iron, who specialized in nickel-plated cast-iron figures, made do with an Ethiopian who was simply a GI in blackface.

By this time, Germany was being identified as the potential enemy of the United States, and dimestore customers were about to be provided with a good contingent of much needed opponents for their nursery-floor American armies. Several makers resorted to using existing figures in a coat of *Wehrmacht* grey or approximate shade. As the Axis threat loomed larger and became reality, Italians and Japanese were supplied, some of them having been on the scene, of course, since the Abyssinia and China campaigns of the thirties.

Finland's courageous fight against the overwhelming odds of Russia in 1939–40 – a brief struggle that caught the world's imagination before it was forgotten in the larger European holocaust – spurred dimestore soldier makers to new heights of internationalism. And sometimes to new depths of colour eccentricity. Barclay, for example, produced a skier in white, meant to be a member of Finland's snow troops who distinguished themselves in the short war; the firm also produced a Russian and, throwing away all the laws of camouflage, painted him red to signify his Communist origins. Red, of course, had been a traditional sign of the 'enemy' in American toy soldiery, a legacy of the Revolutionary struggle against scarlet coated British forces.

The colour was to appear again in the early fifties when some strange Pod Foot troops stomped on to the stage in scarlet jackets, tan helmets and pants – the leaden image of the 'Red Menace' then engulfing Korea. Their sinister mien was deepened by muddy yellow faces and eyes that Barclay reserved for Oriental 'enemy' – slanted type. The eye differed from the normal which had undergone changes between the early thirties and the post-war years, the variations being clues to the age of models for collectors: the earliest Barclay eye was something like an elongated comma on its side, the right being the reverse of the left; in the later thirties it became a dot under a half-moon stroke; by 1950 it had developed into a dot under a straight horizontal stroke. In the matter of eyes at least, one firm showed it had achieved uniformity among its painting crews.

Dimestore makers proliferated, but half a dozen names are revered among specialists such as Richard O'Brien and Don Pielin, who have made a science out of collecting the manufacturers' serial numbers of issues and recording them for fellow collectors.

Barclay, as noted, was the leading prewar maker. It was started in the twenties by an elderly Frenchman, Leon Donze, who sold out to his partner, Michael Levy, about 1932. The figures were distinguished by a tin helmet which was glued and subsequently clipped on. Fighting men were not the only products of the firm: others ranged from ball players to a monoplane and included elaborate hardware such as cannon, mortars and searchlights. Wartime shortages slashed its workforce from 400 to a handful of people, who turned to contract work. After the war the company never regained its former glories, but before its closedown in the early seventies it had the distinction of seeing its Pod Foot survive as about the last of the United States' lead dimestore soldiers.

Manoil soldiers were the brainchild of two brothers, emigrants from Romania, Maurice and Jack Manoil, who started a novelties business in New York in 1928. The soldier side grew out of an original production line that included picture frames, dimestore lamps and giveaway banks. Maurice provided the business muscle for the firm, Jack the creative spark, producing his prototypes through the process of clay sculpture, plaster mould and bronze mould. After a tentative start in Bleeker Street, Manhattan, the firm prospered and moved to bigger premises in Brooklyn. Two wars undermined its fortunes because of metal shortages – the First World War and the Korean war, and the company had experience of shutdowns and fresh starts under slightly altered names. It experimented with

Veterans of Manoil, a highly successful dimestore company: American tin-hatted flag bearers, sold, like most dimestore figures, individually.

composition soldiers and dabbled in plastic, but finally succumbed in the mid-1950s, leaving a huge legacy of collector fodder across the United States.

A number of firms seem to have had seminal connections with Barclay – 'Sons of Barclay', as *Old Toy Soldier Newsletter* calls them. There was All-Nu, based at first in Yonkers, New York, and later in Manhattan, and owned by Frank Krupp who had modelled our old friends Short and Long Stride at the West Hoboken factory. Krupp came from Essen, not from the renowned armaments family, but the son of a goldsmith, therefore to a certain extent he was in the tradition of the old pewterers of Nuremberg and other German tin soldier centres. He never sculpted from sketches but built up his ideas in modelling clay over a wire frame. Ever resourceful, when lead supplies were called up for the war effort after Pearl Harbor, he experimented with cardboard soldiers. His business ended in bankruptcy in 1945. He is remembered, among other contributions, for a marching girls' band that enlivened hundreds of Woolworth's across the United States just prior to the war.

Tommy Toy was one of the few firms that has left its soldiers conveniently marked, under their bases, with its name. It was founded in a parking garage in Union City, New Jersey, in 1935 and lasted a brief three or four years. Involved in the company was Leon Donze, of Barclay fame.

His partners in Tommy Toy included the proprietor of a New York taxi fleet and a medical doctor, surely one of the strangest boards of directors in the history of toy soldiers. Olive Kooken, a sculptress who had designed for Barclay, also worked for Tommy Toy, as well as for another New Jersey dimestore soldier company, American Alloy, of North Bergen. This firm's life was even briefer, little more than a year; it did its modest business COD to avoid bookkeeping and, according to the ever-knowledgeable Richard O'Brien, its end came on the outbreak of war in 1941 when the authorities impounded 30 tons of lead waiting for American Alloy at a rail depot.

There were, too, Grey Iron of Mount Joy, Pennsylvania, founded in 1840, famous for its cast iron men, and still in the general toy business as a division of Donsco, and many other, infinitely shorter lived, companies who trawled the dimestore markets. In the early thirties Lincoln Logs, of Chicago, known for its miniature lumber kits which built up into the cabins dear to the United States' heritage, began to produce 54-millimetre soldiers which have today joined the ranks of prized collectors' items.

North of the border, Canada was usually dependent on British toy soldier imports. In the Second World War, however, with those imports dried to a trickle, a company called London Toy tried to ease the drought with cheap lead figures similar to Manoil and Barclay. About the same time, two brothers, Sam and Ed Breslin, formed United Industries to produce 10-cent soldiers in the American dimestore tradition. The soldier venture lasted only a couple of years until metal supplies ceased, by which time the company was trading in Canada as Breslin Industries. After the war it prospered with desk accessories which its directors found more profitable than soldiers.

No story of American dimestore soldiers is complete without a reference to home casting kits. A number of companies marketed them, aiming at both children and adults. Advertisements carried testimonials from satisfied customers: 'My production is increasing, week by week. Wow! This is the way to make money!' The idea was that every hobbyist could turn into a successful businessman. One catalogue addressed an 'Open letter to Mom and Dad', pressing them to lend their sons money to establish them as entrepreneurs in home foundries and sales of lead soldiers. It was the eternal pursuit of the often attainable, often elusive American dream – through the medium of sizzling hot lead.

CHAPTER **31** NEW, OLD TOY SOLDIERS

The green and gentle Garw valley in south Wales, with the tiny village of Pontycymmer tumbled on its slopes, is a seemingly unmilitary place. It is, however, the source of a remarkable army that calls to the colours several thousand new fighting men every week and sounds the echoes of old imperial glories as far afield as the 'millionaires' supermarket' of Nieman Marcus in downtown Houston. The hallowed halls of West Point contain evidence of Pontycymmer's claim to martial fame, and its men have even penetrated the Academy at Annapolis, *alma mater* of the United States Navy.

Nor is there anything military in the appearance of the two people responsible for all this, Frank Scroby and his wife, Jan, an English couple who have created a cottage industry in the Welsh countryside, producing new toy soldiers in the traditional style of the old makers. By the early 1980s the Scrobys had achieved widespread collector regard for their Blenheim Military Models, with orders flowing in from world renowned stores, commissions from national institutions, and a thriving export business with a 70 per cent emphasis on the United States. But their enterprise has always enjoyed the personal touch that has been one of the success secrets of this talented young couple. It is reflected in the character of their models and in the way they work.

When evening comes to Pontycymmer and bedtime has passed for their young son Glyn – born in 1975 two years after their first prototype 'Blenheim' – Jan often gets to work on one of her master-figures of clay, carving away at the detail with a darning needle 'or anything that comes to hand'. At the same time Frank is busy, as she puts it, with 'his witch's cauldron – adding a bit of this and a bit of that'. But to read into this that theirs is a haphazard business, on catch-as-catch-can lines, would be utterly wrong. It is a professionally run organization that relies on skilful design, precise attention to detail, choice of the best quality materials for the job, efficient utilization of local labour, correct pricing structure and shrewd assessment of markets and demand.

Their aim – like that of many engaged in the commercial or personal production of new toy soldiers – has been to fill the gap caused by the cessation of lead soldiers from the factories of the 'greats'. With Britains' huge army promoted to the ranks of expensive collector items after 1967, few if any military miniatures were made in metal as toys. Specialized modelmakers proliferated, but their creations – exquisitely detailed figures, correct to the last button – had limited function and demand, and were understandably expensive. Above all, in their essential obeisance to accuracy, they lacked the 'toy' look and feel of a faithful Britains or Heyde.

Spurred in many cases by the unique success of Shamus Wade's Nostalgia range (of which more later), fellow Britons and collectors in the United States applied modern methods to the manufacture of soldiers in the visual styles of the toymakers, often for their own pleasure, sometimes for commercial circulation. But in one important respect – cheapness – they could not emulate the old toy soldier: retired for ever was the penny or dimestore warrior. For example, certain Blenheim mounted figures, galloping at £8 apiece to keep pace with inflation, could hardly be regarded in the late seventies as playthings.

The names of the new makers are legion. New ones join their ranks every year. Others, after a brief commercial life, merge or go out of existence. To do justice to them all would require a directory that would be outdated as soon as it was printed. This survey of the rebirth of the toy soldier is mainly confined to three examples of makers – whose work is represented in varying degrees in the *Forbes* Collection. They are the Scrobys and Blenheim of Wales, Wade and his Nostalgia of London,

Examples of Blenheim soldiers are shown in colour in photograph 60. These are by a fellow maker of 'new old toy soldiers', the British firm of Quality Model Soldiers which has produced an effective range of Prussian and French troops of the 1870 war. A wide range of activities is included in the components of each set.

and Harold Pestana, a professor of geology who created a private army in the hills of Maine.

The Scrobys' introduction to lead soldiers was in the early seventies when they had a market stall in the Portobello Road, London, selling old figures to collectors. I remember buying several sets of Britains from them, including a definitive range of the firm's Italian issues brought out originally for the Abyssinian war of 1935; their prices were remarkably reasonable at a time when some other dealers were notably greedy in their attempts to exploit the burgeoning collector interest. In such a wildly accelerating market, fresh stock of old Britains was increasingly hard to come by and the Scrobys turned to experiments in making their own toy soldiers.

At first these experiments were confined to the kitchen stove in their flat in Blenheim Crescent – from which the couple eventually borrowed the name illustrious in British feats of arms. They 'thought Britains' in size, 54 millimetre, and in the universal adoption of the movable arm (although this is attached by a slightly different process in Blenheim soldiers). In 1973 they produced their prototype Waterloo Foot Guard. He was the beginning of their empire.

By the end of a self-employed year they had developed two key aspects of their business that were to be the cornerstones of successful commercial output: a silicon rubber mould used for pre-production, and a top quality metal alloy, rich in tin, akin to that used by jewellers. Whilst being economic, the latter is versatile, amenable to detailed moulding, and safe. When orders began to pour in, the Scrobys looked beyond the high-rent congestion of central London and found the answer in a remote valley in the Welsh hills, where their converted-shop factory provides valuable local employment in an area not renowned for work opportunities.

The Welsh enterprise began in 1975 after the purchase of a pair of terraced cottages for £2500, premises which have since been augmented as the business has grown. Waterloo was followed by the British colonial period which, in turn, developed into a wide range of the British Victorian army, modelled in solid form, painted in gloss and possessing what one collector has called the 'chunky charm' of old toy soldiers. 'The period we are dealing with is when the Victorian army was massive,' says Jan. 'We even market models like the Black Watch cyclists unit: at that time the world thought the bicycle was going to replace the horse!' The Zulu war has been featured dramatically by Blenheim (there is a particularly effective 17th lancer charging at Britain's decisive battle of Ulundi). This is appropriate for a factory based in south Wales, an area which contributed so many names to the 24th of Foot's casualty list at Isandhlwana and the roll of honour in the subsequent heroic defence of Rorke's Drift mission station.

It was, then, perhaps more than coincidence that the British national press turned its attention on the successful man-and-wife industry in the centenary year of the British disaster at Isandhlwana, 1979, at a time when production was passing 2000 figures a week. What fascinated a reporter from *The Guardian* in London was the flexible working system operated by Jan and Frank for their corps of two dozen Welsh ladies employed in the factory, conditions reminiscent of the friendly relationships that existed in Britains' workshops from the earliest days, if not the happy-go-lucky, paint-as-you-like regimen of the Palomeque ladies of Madrid.

Many of the staff are outworkers who take the unpainted soldiers to complete in their homes, but a handful of regulars come in each day, proving, said *The Guardian*, 'that the modern system of flexi-time can work well, even in the country backwaters'. Frank Scroby explained the system: 'We say they must work 40 hours a week, but at what time is up to them. They can come in at 7 a.m. or 11 a.m. – everybody has a key. If one person was slacking the others would soon see it didn't carry on, because it would affect them all. We have such a high standard of work purely because of the relationship we have built up. They really do care.'

Jan Scroby was predicting at that time that 'we have 50 years' work ahead of us'. It certainly seemed no idle boast as one looked at the swelling list of orders, which from time to time include special one-off commissions. In 1976 Blenheim was asked to create a special, large bicentennial set for the Princeton Battlefield Area Preservation Society of the United States. Depicting officers and men of both sides in the War of Independence, it was also issued in a limited edition of 250, and one of these rare sets is in the *Forbes* Museum in Tangier. From West Point Military academy came an order for its colour guard; it was made exclusively for West Point, somewhat to the Scrobys' subsequent regret as they feel they should have afforded it wider circulation by arrangement. Such an arrangement *was* made later when the US Naval Academy at Annapolis commissioned models of its own colour guard. Perhaps the most unusual commission was to follow, however: the Salvation Army ordered a 12-piece band, in modern dress, to be sold through the Army's outlets in Britain, a worthy successor to the famous Salvation band of Britains which has hit astronomic, four-figure prices on the toy soldier collector market. A 1981 contribution consisted of figures of Prince Charles and Lady Diana.

CHAPTER **32** A MATTER OF NOSTALGIA

During their formative years of the seventies in Wales, Jan and Frank Scroby of Blenheim Military Models were closely connected with the Nostalgia figures of Shamus Wade, hailed as the first of the 'new makers'. Under contract, Jan designed the figures and Frank was in charge of production, after Wade had done the research, an arrangement that lasted until 1980. Wade pays high tribute to the skill and lore of Jan Scroby when he discusses the remarkable success of Nostalgia's Mazbhi Sikh of the 32nd Punjab Pioneers, a figure in drab khaki which nevertheless sold out quicker than any others however colourful and ornate were their uniforms: 'Because Jan Scroby knew the history of the Mazbhis, she was able to produce a superb figure with that unique "prickly" look, the result of hundreds of years of being looked down on, combined with fighting ability.'

Significantly, in those words Wade reveals a clue to his own brilliance as an inspirer of new toy soldiers. His approach to the subject is rare indeed – arguably unique – and accounts much for the resounding success in life-like terms of his Nostalgia troops of the British Empire, covering a period from 1850 and 1910. It is best summed up in his own account: 'Of course, research is not just uniform details. Just as important is the type of man, who they were, what they did, physique, complexion etc. Most model soldiers seem to be made from the outside in, i.e. endless research is done to get the uniform right, then a standard figure of a man is fitted into it. With Nostalgia, it is the other way round. First the man is discovered, then the uniform is added.' Thus his Indian Mutiny veterans, paraded at the Delhi Durbar of 1903 – and exemplified in the *Forbes* Collection, not only march with martial pride but with the unmistakable aura of old age; his Fanti woman carrier, baby on back, looks as though she *belongs* to Africa; and many a white officer towers over his colonial troops. No mean philosopher himself, he draws on the views of a colleague collector to argue the case for the new toy soldiers:

When such splendid connoisseur figures are produced today, why produce 'old toy soldier style' figures anyway? Some unkind soul, long ago, when discussing the relative merits of

connoisseur versus toy figures said that the most important thing about a soldier was that he is a member of a group. A person in military uniform, standing alone on a wooden base, is not a soldier – he is someone with halitosis at a fancy dress ball.

The germ of Nostalgia was born 'because I was fed up with the flood of Nazi material that was being published some time ago. . . . I decided it was time someone produced something on the greatest Empire the world has ever known.' A publishing venture involving illustrations of the fighting men of the British Commonwealth and Empire failed – but Nostalgia's 54-millimetre, solid figures followed with enormous success. Between March 1974 and June 1977, 139 completely different figures were produced (650 of each unit). Wade argues that, with the cheapness of modern mould-making techniques, there is no excuse for turning out the same figure, variously painted or with a head or arm change; and after production the moulds are destroyed.

Plans went ahead to produce two regiments of foot (or one of horse) every month, each involving indefatigable research. For years uniform details of one of his obscure targets, the Gibraltarian Carreteros del Rey, evaded him – until Wade found a man who had actually made uniforms for them when an apprentice. Such attention to notably esoteric areas of military activity has inevitably led to keen collector interest in Nostalgia, an interest heightened by the finality of the moulds' destruction. Thus the moon-faced drum and bugle band of the Wei-Hai-Wei 1st Chinese Regiment (a name most military buffs would not know, let alone could pronounce) sold at auction for £200 in 1977, some two years after it was issued at £24.44.

The stories of Blenheim and Nostalgia are both examples of commercial endeavour. Somewhat more private is the story of Harold Pestana, a professor of geology at Colby College, Maine, USA, who spent eight years recreating the variegated strata of British Victorian military life in toy soldier style at his home in the town of Waterville. The result of his labours, which started in 1972, is a unique army of about 1500 figures and pieces, made up of some 130 component sets.

The genesis was a rubber mould he made to copy a Britains' Royal Scots figure which he had picked up in London the year previously. Soon he was busy copying Britains marching figures to create a large parade group of British regiments. 'From the start,' he says, 'I wanted to capture the style or essence of the Britains old lead figures . . . the feeling and charm, and nostalgia of the old toy soldiers, but not to be limited to the castings and types produced by Britains.' In painting he followed the firm's style, but he also uniformed figures of regiments it had never dreamed of: the Pay Corps, the South Wales Borderers, the Dunedin Highland Rifles, and so on.

In the course of this project he found it necessary to create certain figures almost from scratch. Sometimes he decapitated a casting and substituted a new head – as in the case of his Rifle regiments; at other times he fashioned new master figures from which moulds were made – as in the case of the Cameronians.

As Victoria's army grow in his study-workroom, he decided to call his series Soldiers of the Queen, after the famous Boer War song, and house them in uniform red boxes. 'After a long search I found a box manufacturer in Maine and obtained enough boxes for my parade regiments. I got Mr William Miller of the Colby College art department to design a box label for me. The Queen's picture on the label comes from the label on Bombay Gin and while Victoria may not have been amused, it was just the right size!'

His was an enterprise principally for his own satisfaction, producing only very limited issues, although some sets were made for friends and a few were sold through Jock Couts's 'Under Two Flags' shop in London. He says:

Because I was not working commercially, I often did things the hard way. That is, rather than create a new master mould for every figure needed (*a comparatively quick and*

The Royal Engineers balloon unit is a striking (and colourful) contribution to 'new old toy soldiers' by Mark Time of Britain. The figures are solid, in 54mm.

inexpensive process these days, as Shamus Wade has demonstrated), I would often convert an existing casting. Thus, for the Suffolk Regiment celebrating Minden Day I used a seated, armless and headless casting for most of the figures. Heads turned and tilting in various directions were individually glued on, and arms similarly attached. All a very lengthy process, but the result is a large group with no two figures alike as they quaff their anniversary ale, and retaining the charm of the toy soldier.

Eventually he wanted more than just marching figures. Action groups followed. As more and more regiments were produced they included more and more 'original' figures. Standing Indian cavalry were made from a master converted from Britains' Yeoman of the Guard, the Beefeater. Indian infantry firing rifles were derived from plastic Japanese Second World War infantry. Royal Navy sailors firing cannons and Gatling guns were from masters created from Airfix plastic figures; Gatling and Gardner guns came from scratch-built masters. Perhaps the strangest mutation was the Britains' plastic zookeeper who became, through a complex master, a climbing Royal Engineers lineman. In 1980 the *Forbes* Museum of Military Miniatures acquired Harold Pestana's personal collection of Soldiers of the Queen, and there it is preserved. Alongside Blenheim, Nostalgia, Mark Time, British Bulldog, Steadfast, Quality Model Soldiers and the works of similar makers, it represents the new wave of toy soldiers and complements the magnificence of rank upon rank of Britains, Heyde, Mignot, Heinrichsen and the rest.

PART FOUR

Collectors' Legacy

In the *Forbes* Museum of Military Miniatures, the long panoramic scene on the right is made up of Britains with a few conversions and other makes. It represents the British and Imperial armies on campaign in an unnamed terrain some time in the nineteenth century before colourful uniforms vanished from the picture.

What is the *Forbes* Collection of military miniatures. Why does it justify being the illustrative basis of a book on toy armies?

Many other questions may be asked: What makes it different from other collections? Why is it in Morocco? How did it begin? What does it contribute to the science and lore of soldier collecting? Does it include *model* soldiers?

The answers to these and other questions help tell the story behind the establishment in that most international of cities, Tangier, of a million dollars' worth of miniature soldiers and military hardware in a magnificent Moorish palace overlooking the Straits of Gibraltar, where east meets west at the Pillars of Hercules. The *Forbes* Museum of Military Miniatures occupies a huge wing of the Palais Mendoub, once the residence of the Moroccan Sultan's representative in the heyday of Tangier's life as an international port; it is arguably the most exotic, luxurious and spacious setting for a collection of toy soldiers anywhere in the world. Here, veterans of campaign and ceremonial from pre-Roman days to modern times (about 70 000 at time of writing) live in pampered retirement. But the accent is on pageantry rather than war. History is told, not only of the events which inspired the making of these miniature soldiers, but the history of toys themselves. The constant aim of the displays has been to delight the eye and recapture the pleasure invoked by toy soldiers for children of all ages and through the ages.

The army in miniature is the result of the collecting zeal of Malcolm S. Forbes, Chairman and Editor-in-Chief of *Forbes*, the American magazine of business, keen balloon and motor cycle enthusiast, and collector extraordinary. An American of Scottish ancestry, Malcolm Forbes has been the driving force behind the establishment of several rare and valuable collections of works of art on behalf of his company. These collections are dotted around the world.

In the lobby of the firm's Beaux-Arts style building on Fifth Avenue, New York, is to be found a superb collection of Fabergé, including the world's largest private hoard of the master jeweller's Easter eggs, on view to the public at large behind bullet-proof glass; his panelled office sports a Rubens and a Reynolds among other fine paintings. There is also a Fabergé silver model of a paddle steamer, 29 inches long, inscribed 'For the Heir Czarevitch, Alexis Nicolaevitch, from the Volga Shipbuilders'; Forbes loves to watch the delighted reaction of his visitors when he presses a switch and the minutely detailed interior of the priceless vessel lights up and a musical movement plays 'God Save the Czar' and 'Sailing Down the Volga'. Housed in the 1840s town house adjacent to the main building is a superb collection of French military paintings by such luminaries as Meissonier and Detaille.

At the *Forbes* seventeenth-century Chateau de Balleroy in Normandy, the earliest surviving work of the renowned architect François Mansart, is a unique museum of ballooning. At Old Battersea House on the Thames in London, attributed to Sir Christopher Wren and restored at phenomenal expense by the *Forbes* organization, English nineteenth-century painting is represented by a collection of Royal Academy-exhibited works systematically built up by Malcolm's son, Christopher. Another son, Robert – one of five Forbes children – has taken a leading role in the soldier collection and the assembly of some 300 toy tin boats, among them many rare collectors' items, which have their home in the United States.

And at Tangier, the *Forbes* army. Why Tangier? When the Palais Mendoub was acquired in the early seventies in preparation for the launch of an Arabic edition of the fortnightly business magazine, it seemed an innovative gesture of good will to open to the public the *Forbes* Magazine Collection of soldiers, then numbering about 5000. It has since grown enormously in scope and quantity. Forbes employed Robert Gerofi, a brilliant Belgian architect and designer and a Tangier resident, to restore the somewhat run-down palace to its former Islamic glory. Collectors' delights abound in the Palais. For students of Islamic living style they reach their peak in Gerofi's decorations and furnishings of the main salon, or *minzah* – 'room with an outside view', which is glass fronted and looks out across lushly flowering and palm-laden gardens to the sea and southern Spain. Rich green carpets from Rabat cover the floor. Banquettes which line the walls are clad in handwoven fabrics from Fez. There are huge brass tables fashioned in Marrakesh. Carved Chinese elephants, brass-mounted in Morocco, support masses of fresh flowers cut from the palace gardens. To the height of a normal 'living room' wall, the huge salon is tiled in a multi-coloured mosaic of Zellijes design, having more than 1000 pieces to the square yard. But from there the *minzah* soars upward for a further 20 feet or so, culminating in a delicately arched ceiling, the whole of this upper section being carved in snow white plaster by specialists from Fez, the centuries old capital of art and learning in Morocco.

Gerofi's talents are given free reign in the museum – surely the first time that the efforts of a top designer and architect have been directed to the display of a collection of toy soldiers. The museum occupies three spacious ground-floor salons in the main building and a large extension at the corner of the Palais grounds, which has five chambers including a 120-foot gallery overhanging the beach. Modern glazed cabinets, with concealed lighting for maximum viewing effect, are skilfully juxtaposed with Moorish arches and windows of Moroccan leaded glass with their vibrant blues, greens, reds and yellows. Some of the smaller dioramas – for there are several complementing the ranks of *toy* soldiers – gain from being inset, flush, into the plaster walls. (For those attempting emulation, beware: the plaster must be thoroughly dry before any models are placed in position, otherwise the damp encourages lead rot, the scourge of old toy armies.)

Few private collections enjoy the benefits of such spacious and well laid out display facilities, but as collections go, private or public, the *Forbes* army is also remarkable in its scope. Most collectors, or museums with collections of toy and model soldiers, are limited to a certain make, period, or nationality of figures. The *Forbes* Collection cuts across practically all the frontiers of toy and model armies. It embraces all sorts of soldier from the early German flats to modern, connoisseur models correct in every detail. It includes the nineteenth and twentieth century solids and semi-solids by makers such as Heyde and Mignot, and stalwart hollow-cast Britains by the thousand. There is a rare and fascinating injection of leading Spanish makers (Chapter 26), covering the nineteenth century and periods leading up to and subsequent to the Spanish Civil War. One of the few gaps until 1980 was the area of prewar German composition figures – the products of Elastolin, Lineol and similarly based manufacturers. A carefully planned policy of acquisitions was embarked upon in the United States and Europe to repair this deficiency, and now these troops and their wheeled and artillery equipment is represented in large numbers. Similarly, efforts were made to fill another gap – that of American dimestore figures by makers such as Barclay and Manoil.

Composition figures' susceptibility to damp requires that they receive special attention in the sometimes humid climate of northern Morocco. In the early days a few of the Heyde, built of unstable alloys, were beginning to suffer until measures were taken to protect the collection with dehydration crystals obtained in the United States. Use of the chemical amid the Elastolin and Lineol has to be carefully controlled because excessive dryness can be as much a danger to a composition *Wehrmacht* as too much moisture, due to the wire armature's tendency to expand and crack the coating of composition material.

A card index of the collection, begun when the museum was in its infancy in

1974, now covers most known makers of toy soldiers – and many model manufacturers. Appropriately, one of the earliest of the cards to be completed begins: 'Room One, Cabinet 6, The British Army . . . The Life Guards, Britains, No. 1 . . .' In most cabinets Heyde are separated from Britains, Mignot has displays of its own, special attention is given to German composition and Spanish solid figures, flats are housed in the best situations for effect, and semi-solid figures – which are not the most aesthetically pleasing or dramatically displayable of objects – are given a 'lift' by the use of revolving panels like the opening leaves of a book. Thousands of tiny figures need relief, for even the most dedicated observer. An attempt to achieve this has been made by the employment of varying degrees of landscaping, different levels and types of cabinets, a complement of paintings, prints, and posters on military subjects, and the interspersing of dioramas among the ranks of parading and fighting soldiers. Models of the British battleship *Rodney* and the Japanese *Asahi* occupy 12-foot cases.

All is not immediately blood and battle. A brass-bound campaign toilet box with silver fittings announces that it belongs to a captain of the Royal Marines and bears a letter written by its owner in 1853; from a foreign field, he signs it, 'I am, dear Parents, your affectionate Son R. Crowther'. Typical of embroidered samplers sent by serving men to loved ones, and vice versa, is one that reads, 'From Charles to my Dear Mother, Malta, 1911'. For photographic posterity

The first room of the *Forbes* Museum contains two large shipyard models of battleships as well as a representative collection of the great European soldier-makers. The collection occupies a ground-floor wing of the Palais Mendoub and an extension in a large house acquired at the bottom of the palace gardens.

25 000 officers and men form up in a gigantic shape of the Liberty Bell at Camp Dix, New Jersey, in 1918. 'Spy' contributes a cartoon of 'Bobs', Field Marshal Lord Roberts; there is a pencil and charcoal sketch of a man o' war executed in 1893 by Kaiser Wilhelm II, Emperor of Germany. A combat-worn khaki drab tunic bears a label which reads, '101st General Hospital. Staff Sergeant Forbes, Malcolm S. / 35617834'; with it are the medals of the Purple Heart and the Bronze Star, with the latter's citation for meritorious service in Europe in 1944. There is comment on the futility of war. A pencil drawing shows a soldier, bandoliered and holding rifle, under a signpost reading, 'WAR'; a wife holds an apron to quench her tears, beneath another sign pointing to 'WORKHOUSE'. And much unconscious humour of Victorian and Edwardian society.

'Tommy Atkins' Friend' is a gem – a coloured print of an immaculately turned out, long-skirted nurse tending wounded Gordon Highlanders, a lonely and gallant group beset by tribesmen on a mountain peak; the glorious improbability of the incident is overlooked in a flood of Victorian sentiment. In another print, 'The Deserter', a miserable wretch is escorted along a rail platform by two magnificent armed Life Guards, their breastplates gleaming. a child clings to his leg, a wife collapses in shameful tears, comforted by an old woman, a sonorous text proclaims:

> A traitor to his country's laws,
> Of untold woes the unhappy cause –
> O, friends! for one brief moment pause
> To pity the deserter.
>
> His stricken mother, worn with age,
> The young wife's grief tries to assuage.
> But fate has turned a mournful page
> In the life of a deserter.
>
> His little girl in wonder lost
> Tries her dear daddy to accost.
> The thought has ne'er her pure mind crossed
> That father's a deserter.
>
> But he would turn from present pain
> And hope the offender may reclaim
> A better character and name
> Than that of a deserter.

The print – whose known provenance was a London junk shop, then a Chelsea, London, antique market – must rank as the most graphic portrayal of a deserter among any collection of toy soldiers anywhere. A testament of shame, it looms as a dire warning over serried ranks of troops faithfully carrying out their duty in the museum.

More bathos is provided by a framed American songsheet, 'If I'm not at the Roll Call, Kiss Mother Goodbye for Me . . .', accompanied by a drawing of Doughboys waiting to go over the top on the Argonne. And patriotism: First World War posters proclaim, 'Buy Liberty Bonds', 'Make every minute count for Pershing'; another lauds the cosmopolitan nature of the United States' war effort – 'Americans All: Honor Roll: Dubois, Smith, O'Brien, Cejka, Haucke, Pappandrikopolous, Andrani, Villotto, Levy, Turovich, Kowalski, Chriczanevicz, Knutson, Gonzalez.'

Scope and display facilities make the *Forbes* Museum unique. Another distinction it enjoys is a very large component of toys and models representing Muslim fighting men and scenes of Moorish life. In respect for the host country, efforts were made to build up the Islamic content of the museum and the results have opened some new avenues in the field of military miniatures. Thus, when the Moroccan Crown Prince Sidi Mohammed officially opened the museum at an important phrase in its development in August 1978, he could thrill not only as any other boy at such a display of soldiers in miniature, but at the depiction of a decisive victory in his country's history: Edward Surén's diorama of the Battle of the Three Kings (Chapter 36). Significantly, the month represented the 400th anniversary of the battle, which took place about 60 miles away from the site of the museum.

There are extensive sand-table scenes of charging Bedouin horsemen, camel riders and Arabs on foot, many of them the familiar Britains figures – with palm trees from the same source – and some by Heyde, Mignot and other Continental makers. There are desert caravans, Arab street scenes, a school of boys receiving the wisdom of the Koran from an elder, dancing girls, whirling Dervishes besetting an English lancer, Saharan encampments, and traders bargaining for carpets. Vertunni has helped fill the bill for Arab figures, so have Spain's Palomeque and Sanquez. A modern Spanish maker has provided a lancer of the Moroccan Royal Guard, Algerian and Tunisian Spahis and other Arab types. They have company in a palace whose walls are adorned by a multitude of paintings, drawings and etchings of Islamic scenes. In the museum, when the French Foreign Legion appears (usually by courtesy of Britains), it now tends to be heavily outnumbered by Arabs – probably historically accurate but hardly a state of affairs that was reflected on the nursery floors of the western world.

A British model maker, John Ciuffo, has contributed a specially commissioned diorama of the Moroccan people's peaceful 'Green March' into the Spanish Sahara in 1975, an event which contributed to its relinquishment by Spain. His uniquely lifelike figures are made from modelling clay on wire framework. As with other specially commissioned dioramas, the museum curators assisted the research – this time by seeking out and supplying the best coloured news pictures taken of the event, the work of a top international war photographer, British Terry Fincher. The ever topical William Britain would have approved: here was a still-fresh news event providing fodder for model figure making.

From ancient times to present day – and beyond. The collection sets itself no bounds. And on Malcolm Forbes's personal insistence, it is there to be shared, for the museum at the Palais Mendoub, Rue Shakespeare, just beyond Tangier's Kasbah, is open free to the public every day between 10 a.m. and 5 p.m. Written guides to the exhibits are in English, French and Arabic.

CHAPTER **34** PLANNING A BATTLE . . .

The Oxford Dictionary defines the word *diorama* thus:

A mode of scenic representation in which a picture, some portions of which are translucent, is viewed through an aperture, the sides of which are continued towards the picture; the light, which is thrown upon the picture from the roof, may be diminished or increased at pleasure. Also, the building in which such views are exhibited.

In military miniature terms, 'diorama' has through usage come to mean the display of a figure or figures engaged in activity in a representational setting. It can range from a full-scale battle to a single soldier eating his breakfast in the field. The following three chapters examine the planning, assembly and display of two types of diorama to be found in the *Forbes* Museum of Military Miniatures. They have their parallels in many collections.

Both types tackle the problem of presenting large numbers of men, but in different ways. One method employs ready-made toy soldiers, such as tin flats of Germany to depict an eighteenth-century battle in central Europe, or in Britains' figures in an imperial panorama. The other creates a battle scene from Africa in the sixteenth century, made up of custom built figures, part of a special project commissioned from a modern model maker.

There is a room in the *Forbes* Museum at Tangier where time stands permanently at four o'clock in the afternoon of 5 December 1757. The bayonets of the Prussian third battalion of the Garde have smashed through the doorway of the village churchyard of Leuthen, led by Captain Wichard Joachim von Möllendorf, unscathed from the aim of nine Austrian muskets. The number is important. That is what history says. And that is how history is shown in miniature.

About four metres away, representing a mile or so of undulating, snow-dusted landscape dotted by scraggy fir, frozen marsh and sparse meadows, Lieutenant-General von Driesen commanding 35 squadrons of *cuirassiers* and the murderous Bayreuth Dragoons, a picture of disarming elegance in their sky-blue coats, is preparing to engineer the destruction of a cavalry attack with which Austria hopes to save this bitter day.

Around two windmills on a rise overlooking the village, where fighting has raged house by house, in every cattle stall, for every barn and even up to the belfry of the church itself, the Austrian lines are trying to regroup. It is a chaotic scene with disorganized men sometimes ranked 30 deep, sometimes 100, battered and demoralized by the Prussian Frederick's brilliant tactics. The roar of the Prussian artillery is continuous, from the huge 12-pounder battery pieces, or *Brummer**, and smaller cannon which throughout the battle have been horse-drawn or manhandled into the very front line of fighting with devastating effect.

From a position of vantage Old Fritz, Frederick II, King of Prussia, known as the Great, surveys the progress of what history has judged to be the finest of his many victories, the defeat of a battle-hardened professional force three times the size of his own. He sits astride a spirited grey, his shoulders hunched beneath a Prussian-blue coat that bears little insignia to distinguish it from many worn by his officers that day, his beaky nose protruding from beneath an 'army issue' black tricorne hat. His horse has arched neck and one foreleg raised, impatiently. Both horse and rider are as they have been portrayed in contemporary works of Frederick inspecting the Garde, and as Johann Gottfried Hilpert, toy soldier maker of Nuremberg, cast them in tin around the year 1777. In this microcosm of an eighteenth-century battle in Silesia, however, Frederick and mount are the production of Alloys Ochel of Kiel, the twentieth-century maker of tin flats who, like others, could find no better inspiration than Hilpert's master figure when modelling Old Fritz.

With the 30-millimetre figure of Frederick on this battlefield are some 7000 similar sized flats by Ochel, Heinrichsen and other makers. The respective numbers of the Prussians and Austrians, 4000 and 3000, do not reflect the relative sizes of the two armies engaged that day but concentrate on Frederick's hour of victory as he poured his strength into the fray. Few dioramas can ever use the full complement of soldiers that took part in a particular battle: units arrive on the scene after others; some depart; some are decimated, or eliminated before the dramatic sequence chosen for depiction. Space has its limits. The Austrians' original line at the Battle of Leuthen was nearly five miles long. In their moves after the first shots – feint, approach march, attacks around and in Leuthen, final breakthrough and pursuit – some of Frederick's men covered fully 12 miles. To show, in miniature, the complete terrain and the total number of men involved on both sides, approximately 120,000, would not only need a large swathe of the

Brummer was the affectionate name given to these guns by the Prussian army. Thomas Carlyle translates it as 'Bellowers' or 'Boomers'; the latter is probably nearer the onomatopoeic connotation of the word.

Forbes Palais Mendoub and its grounds, but much of the scene would be unexciting, if not boring. To concentrate time, action and interest is the thing. To this end the diorama, in one large L-shaped plan, presents the bloody struggle for Leuthen village and the beginnings of the action that smashed the Austrian cavalry, both dramatic peaks of the battle. In showing them both as apparently concurrent events, it takes a little licence in time (less than an hour, in fact), as they happened in reality consecutively. Likewise, a little licence in distance is taken for the convenience of the viewer.

Work began on the *Forbes* diorama of Leuthen, a battle of the Seven Years' War, on a crisp Saturday morning in December 1978, in a large room above the Maximilianstrasse in Munich. The 'furniture' might have been disconcerting had this not been the storeroom of an auction house and dealer, Graf Klenau, specialist in militaria, arms and armour. Tailor's dummies stood clothed in the black and silver of the SS. Nazi helmets were stacked in heaps like grey melons. Swastika banners draped the walls. The Führer and his gang stared hard from signed photographs. Insignia and regalia abounded, the glittering detritus of the Third Reich. Welcome relief was provided by the dress uniform and helmet of a station master – a Weimar railman's Sunday best – by far the most impressive livery in the collection.

As curators of the Palais Mendoub museum, Anne and I were in Munich to inspect some thirty-odd thousand German tin flats, and 1300 Heyde (repainted in 1914 and Weimar Republic parades by Major Willy Lang), purchased for the collection in a private deal with Graf Klenau. The provenance of this interesting consignment was the Wehrgeschichtliches Museum at Schloss Rastatt, near Karlsruhe, West Germany, an army history museum which had decided these figures were now surplus to its requirements, having had them on display for many years.

Wartime upheaval and post-war reorganization had accounted for the disposal of these tin soldiers and such a background is not conducive to the maintenance of accurate records, as we found when we delved into the battery of crates that housed the collection. We knew that they contained the components for a diorama of the Battle of Leuthen – which had been on display at Rastatt many years ago – and it was easy to separate these from the rest of the flats, boxed sets of lovely old Heinrichsens and a huge mass (possibly 20 000) of Ochel, Neckel and other makers' figures of the German army in Africa in two world wars. But there were no written accounts or drawn details of the way the diorama had been composed and application to the Wehrgeschichtliches Museum produced some helpful, but sparse, information in general terms and a short list of book references on Frederick the Great's campaigns.

Apart from a preponderance of loose figures, however, there were some groups of soldiers – cavalry and infantry – still attached to the white paper (representing snow) on which they had been mounted in the diorama. On the paper of a few of these a provident museum servant had scribbled the title of the unit – Pannwitz, Alt-Braunschweig, Harrach, Bayreuth, and so on. When such groups existed in the strength and formation of platoons, the basic tactical unit of the Prussian infantry, the three ranks were staggered and thus 'locked on' for fire, and they were accurately flanked by lieutenants and NCOs, with more NCOs and an officer supporting from the rear.

This was a comforting discovery; it meant that, working in the near-dark as we were, any assumptions or conclusions could be made in the knowledge that whoever set up the diorama in the first place knew what he was doing. Similarly, it soon became evident that uniform details painted on the Prussians and Austrians were authentic. Time, patience and research were all that was needed to complete the jigsaw.

The key piece of the Leuthen jigsaw was the answer to the question: what

By the thousand they play their role in the diorama of the Battle of Leuthen. Detached from the mélée, in close-up are two Prussian cuirassiers by Ochel.

phase of the battle is depicted? It lasted little over four hours, encompassing the whole of an afternoon until winter darkness overtook the field. (At one point an anxious aide had ridden up to Frederick, watch in hand, to warn that there remained only four hours of daylight; but the precisely drilled Potsdamers obliged punctually, clearing the field of opposition before nightfall!) As in any battle, there was a series of actions, but at Leuthen the most dramatic, the most likely candidate for reproduction in two or three dimensional art, was, of course, the fight around the village itself. And here, at the bottom of a crate, lay tangible proof that the heart of the diorama was just that: we found a model of Leuthen village church, its tower and belfry not yet reduced to the ruin they subsequently experienced on that day, its walled yard still bearing evidence of its defenders in a few adhering figures.

Deeper investigation and cataloguing of the figures had to wait, however. Space was needed for that and it was available at the Palais Mendoub in Tangier, the collection's ultimate destination. There in a large and sunny penthouse room atop the palace we were able to lay out the two armies for inspection and a network of 20-centimetre square floor tiles provided an ideal grid on which to plan the eventual battle table. Actual installation had to await the building of a museum extension, which had been embarked on partly in order to house the huge Rastatt acquisition. In the meantime research could go ahead at the museum in Rastatt, at the Bayerischen Armeemuseum in Ingoldstadt, West Germany, which has a similar diorama, at the National Army Museum in London, through the works of authorities ranging from Thomas Carlyle to the contemporary Christopher Duffy, and with the aid of certain collectors, notably the ever-helpful Frederician student, Remigio Gennari of Rome. And the essential basis of the research, of course, was a knowledge of what exactly happened on the afternoon of 5 December 1757.

Two days before the battle of Leuthen, as the Prussian army reached Neumarkt on its eastward march into Silesia, Frederick made clear to his commanders his intention of attacking the Austrians wherever they could be found. He is said to have inspired hardened veterans to tears of enthusiasm by warning 'if any regiment of cavalry shall fail to crash straight into the enemy, when ordered, I shall have it dismounted immediately after the battle and turned into a garrison regiment. If any infantry battalion so much as wavers, it will lose its colours and its swords, and I shall have the braid cut from its uniform.' There was no doubt how the Prussian army was going to act in the coming fight.

Summarized, for history and the diorama maker, this is the timetable of events on 5 December:

The Austrian army, fortified by abatis, redoubts, trenches, ditches and many felled trees, is drawn up in a line four to five miles long, stretching from the hamlets of Nippern in the north to Sagschütz in the south, with the large village of Leuthen at the left centre. The field before it is undulating, seamed by a few roads and dotted with clumps of fir. A few windmills on rises and churches – like the one at Leuthen ringed by stout churchyard walls – provide the only reasonable viewpoints.

The first action comes near the hamlet of Borne, an advance post of the Austrians in front of their right centre. In the half light of early morning, Austrian dragoons and hussars are repulsed; a minor action, but fringe benefits to the Prussians include the mortal wounding of General Nostitz and the capture of an entire field bakery with the morning's batch of bread intact.

Foxy Frederick now executes a brilliant move. He divides his four columns into two and heads them south behind the cover of a series of low ranges – out of sight of the Austrians, who can be forgiven for believing he has opted for disengagement. Then at the north – on the Austrian right – he launches a feint attack, which so unnerves the Austrian incumbent general, Lucchesi, that he screams for reserves to be sent to his help. On his third desperate appeal ('If cavalry do not come, I will not be responsible for the issue'), the Austrian commander-in-chief, Prince Charles of Lorraine, allows masses of horse and foot to be sent north, away from the very area where deadly danger is going to come. For Frederick, having marched south on a line parallel to the enemy front, is now ready to turn left and strike at the Austrian left centre. It is one o'clock in the afternoon and the sun glistens on the battlefield's coating of light snow.

He punches home the attack with his famed oblique order, blocks of infantry moving stairwise, or in echelon. From a standing line, the first battalion starts to march; after it has gone 50 paces, the next battalion on the left moves off, and so on. According to Archenholtz, an eighteenth-century writer on military tactics, troops moving like this show to the enemy what appears to be 'a totally chaotic mass of men heaped on one another, but it needs only that the commander lift his finger; instantly this living coil of knotted intricacies develops itself in perfect order, and, with a speed like that of mountain rivers when the ice breaks, is upon its enemy.'

The Prussian attack smashes into the least reliable units of the Austrian front, Württembergers, who break. 'Our army advanced with sounding music, as if on parade,' said a corporal of the advance guard. Gunners with horse teams are up there in the van, pounding the Austrian lines at point blank range, hitching up, moving forward, and firing again. Croat musketeers in ditches, fir clumps and frozen marshes are winkled out. Frederick's cavalry, on the right, repulses a fierce Austrian counter attack by Nadasti's dragoons.

Too late now, Prince Charles realizes he has fallen into a trap by sending his reserves north to support Lucchesi. They are hurriedly rushed south to bolster the Austrian left, now based on the houses and the church of Leuthen village. Prussian victory comes there when Möllendorf's Garde storms the high walls, their commander bellowing: 'Follow me, whoever is a man!'

An Austrian infantry officer, the Prince de Ligne, describes the confusion in his army:

The Austrian regiment Andlau, at our right hand, could not get itself formed properly by reason of the houses; it was standing thirty deep and sometimes its shot hit us in the back. On my left the regiment Merci ran its ways; and I was glad of that, in comparison. By no method or effort could I get the dragoons of Bathyani, who stood fifty yards in rear of me, to cut in a little, and help me out – no good cutting hereabouts, think the dragoons of Bathyani. My soldiers, who were still tired with running, and had no cannon [these either from necessity or choice they had left behind], were got scattered, fewer in number, and were fighting mainly out of sullenness.

Austria now tries to regroup on the windmill heights overlooking Leuthen, but the battle is practically decided. Lucchesi, abandoning his position of redundancy in the north, launches a cavalry attack on the seething left flank of the Prussian infantry. But von Driesen is there, with his cuirassiers and dragoons concealed by a low rise. They crash into the Austrian cavalry's flank. Lucchesi is killed. The Austrian rout towards Lissa begins as dusk falls on the blooded snow.

In presenting a diorama which employs *toy* soldiers instead of custom-built figures – in this case, 30-millimetre flats which are almost two-dimensional – compromise is constant. For one thing, the diorama cannot be viewed in the round as a specially commissioned example may be. Nothing is more ineffective than viewing a mass of flats 'end on': it looks like a forest of thin metal spikes. An L-shaped plan was considered the most efficient means of displaying the battle and the figures were arranged so that they can be seen to maximum advantage by an observer standing in the angle of the L. It became clear that the original diorama in

The Moroccan people's peaceful 'Green March' into the Spanish Sahara is captured in microcosm in the plasticine-like figures of British diorama maker John Ciuffo, one of several of his displays in the *Forbes* Collection.

Rastatt had been designed to be viewed unilaterally, as some of the figures were painted only on one side. A few others had a curious dual role: on one side they were painted as Prussian, on the other Austrian. The choice was ours.

To complete the Battle of Leuthen we needed sound: the crash of artillery, the rattle of musketry, men's shouts, whinnying horses, the rumble of waggons, and martial music. This was provided by a tape built up from parts of a recording of battle sound effects mixed together in realistic ways.

Leuthen village was constructed in London, from wood and card, working on German architectural books and plans and photographs of the Bayerischen Armeemuseum diorama. From London, too, came 250 specially commissioned fir trees, appropriately scraggy, fences, felled trees, snow powder and other scenic effects. A German scenic backdrop for model railways was converted to snow-dusted Silesia of the eighteenth century. (Blue skies, with some cloud? Fortunately, yes. One account records that the sun came out, dispelling the mist, shortly before the main fighting began.) Plaster-type landscaping was done *in situ*. Then the armies were placed. It was, of course, a glorious excuse to enjoy playing with toy soldiers.

Just as much fun has been the planning of other panoramic displays using ready-made toy soldiers. One 20-foot long cabinet in the museum employs about 1000, mainly Britains (including a few conversions, with an injection of a few modern makes), on campaign in a notional terrain some time in the middle to late nineteenth century. The idea was to present toy soldiers as such. Therefore, from a dioramic point of view, accuracy takes second place to visual effect, as cavalry in their parade-ground review uniforms are joined in the field by skirmishing infantry in red tunics and white sun helmets.

This is the British and Imperial army before it was swallowed by anonymous khaki drab. The enemy is unspecified – somewhere out there ahead of the line infantry advance guard and the hussars. Because the nature of the display is to show *toys*, a little licence in the mix of makers is taken, with here and there a platoon of Heyde amid the Britains; after all, what small boy didn't mix his

Spacious setting for dioramas: they occupy the central part of this room at the museum, Edward Surén's Battle of the Three Kings on the left, beyond it a Napoleonic battle scene made up from German flats.

soldiers that way? Scenic realism stops short at a painted mountain backdrop, plywood contours painted sandy-brown, and some rock outcrops and sand provided by Tangier beach. Behind the forward troops there are support infantry marching at the slope, squadrons of lancers and dragoons, medical corps with horse ambulances and tents, mountain artillery, naval landing parties with quick firers and 4.7s, Highlanders, Indians and camel troops, supply waggons, galloping horse artillery, and sharpshooters amid the crags: a cross section of Britains' catalogue in its heyday. A private collector's conversion from Britains – a Royal Engineers' observation balloon unit – adds a touch of 'modern' technology to the display of anachronistic glories. This is not a diorama. Neither the scenic effects nor the uniforms and postures of the figures are realistic enough to make that pretension. It is, given the space, a way of displaying a toy soldier collection somewhat differently than marshalling it in ranks upon shelves.

Similarly, the museum has used 700 flats by Ochel of Germany to create an imaginary battle scene of the Napoleonic wars in Europe. The scene basically represents the siege of a Prussian-held farm by the French, with Scottish Highland troops advancing in an attempt to relieve their hard-pressed allies. As the battle is hypothetical, licence has been taken in some of the types of troops employed; the full variety of units and uniforms would not have been found in any single action. In the same way, distance has been compressed to accommodate the collection in a cabinet seven feet long by three feet wide. Landscaping goes farther than in the case of the Britains' panorama, but does not reach the realistic heights of the Battle of Leuthen. Napoleon and Marshal Soult are there; there are a party of general staff, a member of the Emperor's Italian guard of honour and a Mameluke standard bearer of the Imperial Guard; a Prussian general, possibly Blücher, pipe in hand, discusses the battle with two British general officers; in the field between the two staffs infantry and cavalry slog it out. The aim has been to present flats for the purpose for which they were designed – to give the maximum amount of pleasure to the eye.

The 20 000-strong contingent of Germans in Africa, found in the Rastatt acquisition, presented a diorama problem of a different kind because of the vast numbers. Split roughly half and half between the two world wars, one needed bush terrain of East Africa and the other the characteristic landscape of the Western Desert. The latter presented no difficulty whatsoever as ample supplies of sand lie at the bottom of the cliff beneath the museum's galleries. Neither war, with its German field grey, colonial drab or desert yellow, presents such a colourful mix of uniforms as Leuthen or the Napoleonic era, but dramatic effect is achieved by the large numbers involved.

When, in 1979, I raised in the British magazine, *Military Modelling*, the mystery of some black-faced soldiers found sitting in the half-track vehicles of Rommel's Western Desert Afrika Korps (maker, possibly Neckel), Remigio Gennari in Rome wrote to suggest they were most likely the Italian Libyan troops of General Malitti's armoured and mechanized division. But these forage-capped, or sun-helmeted soldiers often appear to be sitting among *German* crews. Surely, the Afrika Korps would not have mixed the Libyan auxiliaries of Italy with its own personnel? And the Germans themselves employed no black troops in the Western Desert campaigns of the Second World War.

The fascinating theory still remains that when Nazi hopes of pan-African domination were at their brightest, the toy soldier makers pressed into *Wehrmacht* service black African troops, just as the conquering generals inevitably would have done if Hitler's penetration into Africa had succeeded. Once the deliberate mistake had been committed, it could easily have been perpetuated by post-war makers in Germany. If this story of misplaced German hopes is the right one, then these 'hybrids' have at last found a campaigning part to play in North Africa – on a sand table in Morocco.

CHAPTER **36** HISTORY FROM SCRATCH

When a diorama is commissioned from a modelmaker and the commission is a wholly accurate representation of an event and the setting in which it took place, there can be no short cuts. We are not now dependent on the faithfulness to reality of the original toy soldiers. There can be no question of compromise on account of the material available. This is history from scratch, and the full responsibility rests on the modelmaker. When the modelmaker is Edward Surén the responsibility for accuracy is something of a religion.

Surén's 30-millimetre solid figures had already achieved an international reputation among collectors in the seventies when Malcolm Forbes began to order dioramas from him. Surén has always called them Willie figures, a term which derives from his wartime association with the Eighteenth Cavalry in India (a regiment that was the result of the 1922 amalgamation of the 6th Bengal Cavalry and the 7th Hariana Lancers). Because of Surén's modest stature and characteristic moustache, his fellow officers likened him to Little Willie, son of the Kaiser in the previous war; the 'Little' grew into disuse, however, when, in Surén's words, 'some undeserved promotion seemed to give me added stature'. 'Willie' remained.

In 1977 Forbes asked Surén to cast around for a suitable and substantial battle diorama subject of Moroccan interest, a model that would make a significant contribution to the Morrish content of the museum in Tangier. The answer was found in a suggestion from Robert Gerofi, the architect-designer who had replanned and refurbished the Palais Mendoub and its museum. There was, he pointed out, a momentous battle in Moroccan history which took place on 4 August 1578, and in which the forces of Islam soundly defeated those of Don Sebastian, the Catholic King of Portugal. It is variously known as the Battle of el-Ksar el-Kebir, the Battle of Oued el Makhazen (from the town and the river near which it took place) and – more popularly – the Battle of the Three Kings (from the three main protagonists).

Although Moroccan schoolchildren learn of the battle and study its implications in their lessons, European textbooks pay little attention to this defeat for Christianity, such is the partiality of history teaching. Records, other than in Arabic, are therefore sparse. And although Surén's research subsequently led him to highly specialized depositories of learning in several countries, the first breakthrough came from a most unacademic source. Browsing through a Moroccan holiday brochure, handed out to visitors at the state's tourist office in Regent Street, London, my wife and I came across a definitive account of the battle, occupying five pages and illustrated with examples of the dress worn by combatants and a contemporary sketch plan of the action. For Surén it was a start – even though there were to be many more months of research before the first of more than 600 figures could be designed. At least, the account told what had happened.

Don Sebastian, the child-king of Portugal, nursed an ambitious dream to become the first Christian emperor of Morocco. In 1574 he judged the time was ripe to achieve his wish to 'ruin Morocco and grind the adepts of the Moslem faith in the mill of debasement', according to the Moroccan historian En-Naciri Es Slawi. Ignoring the prudent warnings of his uncle, Philip II of Spain, he thrust out with a small army from the coastal enclaves of Ceuta and Tangier, but within a few months retired from Morocco after an inauspicious encounter with the forces of the reigning Sultan, Moulay Mohammed.

While Don Sebastian brooded and planned for another invasion, Morocco was rent by internal dissension. Moulay Mohammed was displaced by the intrigues of his uncle, Abd-el-Malek, who seized the throne by force of arms. Mohammed fled and, *in extremis*, turned to his erstwhile enemy, Don Sebastian, to form an alliance. To the Portuguese king he made wild promises of Moroccan territory in return for military aid. With the hollow styling of 'Emperor of Morocco' and Mohammed's conferred rights 'to teach the faith of Jesus Christ in Barbary', Don Sebastian, still in his early twenties, returned to Africa with 40 000 Portuguese, Spanish, German and Italian troops and a 6000-strong Papal contingent. They were joined by 6000 Moors under the former Sultan. The morning of 4 August 1578, a day of suffocating heat, found the 'Three Kings' – Don Sebastian with Moulay Mohammed, and Sultan Abd-el-Malek – facing each other on rolling ground near the V-junction of the Makhazen and Loukkos rivers, 60 miles south of Tangier.

Amply supported by artillery, Abd-el-Malek's army of 15 000 professionals, 44 000 militia and additional tribesmen, was not weighed down with non-

Bowlers in position, umbrellas at the ready, modelmaker Edward Surén (*centre*) and colleagues prepare for the annual memorial parade of cavalry regiments in Hyde Park, London. In dioramic terms, Surén says: 'If you want a battle from me, you get it . . . blood, rape, the lot.'

Preparatory sketch by
Surén for the Battle of
the Three Kings (*see
the diorama in colour* in
photographs 75 to 78).
and one of the old
prints that inspired his
model figures of the
Portuguese army.

combatants. On the other hand, carts carrying, women, children, servants, priests and nuns, and even huge altars to be set up in the field, accompanied the host of Don Sebastian, who had taken with him a gilded carriage for the triumphal entry into Fez. Rich were the pickings and bloody the results, therefore, when the Moroccans broke through into the soft heart of the Portuguese formation after four hours of fighting that began at high noon.

A crescent shaped attack, supported by bombardment, split Don Sebastian's infantry in two. His cannons ran out of ammunition. Lords and ladies, priests and nuns fled in panic, many to drown in the Makhazen, as 'the troops fell in a heap one upon another as sheaves of wheat fall before a scythe. . . .' In the hour of Morocco's triumph all three kings were united in death. Don Sebastian, who had three horses shot beneath him, was struck down by a Moor's scimitar. Moulay Mohammed, fleeing for his life, drowned in the tidally swollen river; his corpse was recovered, skinned, stuffed with straw and paraded through the town bazaars of Morocco. Abd-el-Malek, whose troops were the victors, was robbed of the fruits of success by a Spanish renegade who served him a poisoned cake in his tent, where he died before the battle's climax.

Armed with this background knowledge, Surén sent out his research feelers from his battle headquarters in London – a narrow, book-lined study, the desk littered with cutting tools, drawings and plans, a shelf above it laden six-deep with Willie master figures from a hundred battles. Terrain and accoutrements were two obvious areas of research. Among the latter, the colourful arms and standards of the Portuguese leaders and their cohorts demanded special attention. In Lisbon, Edward Surén pressed his brother into service. Blanks were struck at several museums and at the apparently promising Cabinete de Estudos de Heraldica, a sort of college of arms. In the heraldic department of the Museu Militar, Lisbon, however, a valuable ally was found in the director, Captain Paiva Couceiro, who called in the help of a retired, former director, Lieut-Colonel Campos e Sousa in Oporto. Their considered view was that by the time of the battle, commanders in the field no longer carried their personal standards. Instead the army was grouped into regiments, each having its own standard. From Lisbon, piece by piece, month by month, gems of information were transmitted back to Surén in London or in the summer retreat of his house at Eze on the Middle Corniche in the south of France. . . .

Don Sebastian took the field initially in his coach. He wore a chased and richly damasked helmet, and a new suit of armour over which was worn a tabard of St Louis. Behind him came the royal standard. Abd-el-Malek rode slowly on to the field on a magnificent charger preceded by mounted drummers and followed by mounted trumpeters. Over his head was borne the royal umbrella of crimson and gold carried by an attendant (the Sultan, who was in ill health, later was seen exhorting his troops from a litter). Five standard bearers carried green banners of Islam and there were many other standards of the Maghreb saints, of every colour and shade, some fashioned in silk, others velvet, embroidered in gold brocade. . . . Surén's practised eye noted the information and underlined salient points for potential use in the diorama.

Details of the Portuguese artillery, wagons and magnificent campaign tents were built up from museum and book sources. In London the British Museum and the Institute of African and Oriental Studies provided useful information about the sixteenth-century attire of Berbers and other tribes. Captain Couceiro found a print of an eye-witness's sketch of the battle; it showed the Moorish crescent-shaped attack like the sweep of a bull's horns, gave little help on uniforms which appeared remarkably similar on both sides, but provided an unexpected bonus by depicting clearly an array of Portuguese standards. A flood of preparatory battle sketches began to engulf Surén's desk, Moroccan stick-men in black ink, Portuguese in red.

In the summer of 1977 there came a helpful despatch from his man 'in the field', Robert Gerofi who had accompanied a Jeep-borne expedition to the scene of the fight, led by former minister and newspaper owner Moulay Ahmed Alaoui. The occasion was the 399th anniversary of the battle and it produced full newspaper accounts in French and a series of photographs of the terrain and of the River Makhazen, running between brown, parched banks. Although the area is still in open country and largely uncultivated, there have been important changes. Working on contemporary accounts, translated from Arabic and Portuguese, Surén decided that a more natural and truthful guide for his landscaping was a watercolour painted by his wife, Sonia, some thousands of miles away across the world. A dusty river-bed scene in India seemed to capture the appearance and atmosphere of the Moroccan waddies that were the site of carnage in 1578.

When Edward Surén and his Battle of the Three Kings finally moved to Tangier they went as a passenger on a Royal Air Maroc flight and 19kg, or 40lb, of special baggage – the 600-odd figures, cannon and carriages that made up the scene. He had shipped, ahead, the five-foot square diorama base on which basic landscaping had placed the Oued Makhazen between its banks. In the Palais Mendoub he completed the base landscaping and placed each, carefully pre-painted, piece in position.

The moment depicted is that of breakthrough by Abd-el-Malek's triumphant horde. A spearman on a huge camel leads the van of the Moroccan cavalry, a long green pennant fluttering on his lance. In the Moorish advance guard the red flags with silver crescents mingle and contrast with the crosses of the Portuguese banners. As a line of supply wagons is engulfed, their guards fight back bravely, ignored by the Portuguese cavalry which is still desperately trying to stem the enemy's advance. Dead and injured lie in numbers, their blood mingling with the sand, some of the wounded being finished off by the swords and spears of tribesmen. In the mainly abandoned camp of Don Sebastian servants have turned to the ransacking of treasure and women – 'If you want a battle from me, you get it . . . blood, rape, the lot,' says Surén. In the Moroccan lines huge, fabulously turbanned drummers beat brass mounted drums atop caparisoned camels, backed by a support group of trumpeters and cymbalists on mules. Nuns flee amid maddened, bolting horses. A lonely group of bishops waits bravely in prayer at an altar set up in the field as only a thin shield of four lines of swordsmen and musketeers stand between it and the Moors. All around, troops are beginning to break and flee. In the muddy waters of a plastic liquid river – 'it took four or five coats' – Moulay Mohammed drowns alone as his horse bolts to safety up the bank. Elsewhere Don Sebastian dies with his hopes. The death of Abd-el-Malek, of poison in his tent, could not be shown, says Surén, because it happened too far away from the scene of action covered by the diorama.

There was a sequel to the Battle of the Three Kings and this, too, has its place in the *Forbes* Museum Collection. In 1590 at an action known as the Battle of Songhai, soldiers and tribesmen of the northern Nigerian states met the forces of the Moroccans and tried to surprise and defeat their opponents by suddenly emerging from behind large herds of cattle they were pushing ahead of them. But the surprise was on the Nigerians. They were unaware that the Moroccans were equipped with firearms captured from the Portuguese at the Battle of the Three Kings and during the mopping-up aftermath in northern Morocco. Although some 12 years old, these firearms had a devastating effect on the hapless Nigerians and victory was assured for the Moroccans.

For Malcolm Forbes, Edward Surén undertook to produce a diorama of Songhai, comprising about 600 foot and mounted figures, cattle and palm trees. When these words were being written the Surén studio table was being invaded by a motley herd of bony, long-horned cows, and photographs of northern Nigeria lay among diagrams of bovine dissections. 'I've had the devil's own job making this camel,' said Surén. 'When a camel's lying down, its leg folds peculiarly in three places. You can't see it when the model's completed, because the leg's underneath the camel's body. But for me, I've just got to know it's *right*.'

CHAPTER **37** KEEPING THE TROOPS HAPPY

Many a collection of lead toy soldiers, dating from as far back as 70, 80 or even more years ago, reveals a near-mint condition when the lids of the cardboard boxes are lifted and the original brown tissue paper wrapping is removed. The soldiers would appear hardly to have been out of their boxes – and that, more than coincidentally, could have been an important part of the reason why they have survived in such healthy, robust condition with the bloom still fresh and clear on their paint.

For lead soldiers, tough campaigners that they are, are susceptible to two scourges, sunlight and damp. Storage in their original cardboard boxes would have kept them away from sunlight which can affect their paint. At the same time, any wrapping materials with a tendency to absorb moisture – such as tissue paper and cardboard – would have helped to prevent reactions in the metal which are exacerbated by damp in the atmosphere.

David Borthwick, the toy and model soldier specialist at the London headquarters of Phillips, the auctioneers, reckons that 'anyone who can remember his O level chemistry can tell you how to look after a lead army'. Thus armed (and fortified by the experience that comes from handling several thousand figures pouring into the auction room every week), he has co-operated with the British collector, James Opie, to write a short treatise on soldier-care, which the latter has used in his periodic part-work, *The Encyclopedia of British Toy Soldiers*.

They advise that simple preventive measures are the best cure for what collectors know as lead rot, or lead disease, the dreaded ailment that can turn a battalion of soldiers into ignominious piles of grey dust unless checked. And the advice is based on basic knowledge of what makes a toy soldier: usually lead for 'good flow and bendability'; tin for strength; and antimony – generally $12\frac{1}{2}$ per cent in Britains – which encourages the alloy to expand into the mould when cooling, giving a crisp, well-finished casting.

Lead, however, can cause reactions between the lead and sulphurous impurities in the atmosphere. An ionic exchange at molecular level results in the reduction of exposed lead into lead sulphide, recognized by its grey, powdery appearance. Various organic compounds can also cause this. Mothballs are an insidious menace to lead soldiers. So are cabinets made of oak, which are liable to give off acidic fumes. Too much handling of figures is bad for them because of the natural acid salts in our hands. The trouble begins with a characteristic rough touch to the metal. At its worst, it can work right through the figure and, if allowed to complete its process, reduce it to grey dust.

Reaction takes place only when the metal is in contact with impurities. (Incidentally, a figure coming into contact with a metal pin in a display cabinet can lead to corrosion.) Once the necessary conditions for reaction are removed, the cause of the trouble, lead sulphide, is stable and cannot spread to other models. That is why prevention is the best cure.

Sulphides dissolve in water and become sulphuric acid. Damp, therefore, is the greatest enemy. Lead soldiers should be stored or displayed in the dryest atmosphere possible. In display, drying crystals should be used; in the *Forbes*

Collection they are usually camouflaged, inside a tent, behind modelling lichen undergrowth, or in a strategic pile of rocks. There should be ventilation – if this will help fight damp (hardly the answer in an excessively humid climate); and if ventilation is employed there should be filters to keep out dust, which, in time, can detract from the permanent appearance of toy and model figures.

Plastic wrapping, which encourages condensation, should not be used in storage. Better the original cardboard box and damp-absorbent tissue paper, obviously of the non-acid variety if this is possible. Excessive dryness, however, *can* be harmful to composition soldiers of the Elastolin-Lineol variety by causing shrinkage of the material. At the same time, the humidity must be balanced because excessive moisture can cause the wire armatures inside the figures to corrode, expand, and split their bodies.

The paintwork of figures demands attention to a different set of rules. Paint deteriorates in sunlight: I have come across collections in which figures are dulled on one side but still have their original bloom on the other simply because this is how they have been exposed to strong light – probably sunlight – for a long period. Museums are traditionally encouraged to avoid daylight lighting, a luxury which is not always available to them. Similarly, extremes of heat or cold, which may be harmless to the metal content of figures, can easily and quickly cause paintwork to become discoloured or to flake.

What does a collector do if he or she is faced with bad cases of lead disease in the army? Three methods are available. Two of them, the electrochemical and the acid treatment, require expert and experienced operation and could not possibly be entertained by an amateur. A third method involves treatment of the affected figures with ion-exchange resin. It is a relatively simple process, but here again, the sound advice of a chemist should be obtained. In the end, it is prevention that counts. A happy atmosphere and not too much campaigning in burning sunlight works wonders for your armies.

CHAPTER 38 THE LAST ROUND

The entrance porch to the present-day Britains' factory in Blackhorse Lane, north-east London, is flanked by Union Jack murals. They looked particularly bright on a cold and grey afternoon late in 1980, even though the printed 'No vacancies' sign hanging on the door was evidence of a bleak economic climate outside. International toy firms had been going through lean times in the preceding six months, but inside Britains there was a cheerful bustle that spoke of full order books and confidence.

'It's a funny thing, but we seldom get time to think about the past,' said Roy Selwyn-Smith, managing director, leafing through two box files of yellowing photographs and press cuttings. To the visitor, the only visible obeisance to a lead-soldier heritage is a cased example of the Royal State Coach, made for the 1953 coronation of Elizabeth II, and placed modestly in the entrance hall.

The showroom, where trade buyers are regaled with established and new products, is a Santa Claus grotto lined with dazzlingly colourful farms, cowboys, zoos, soldiers, agricultural equipment and vehicles, much of it detailed to a degree unheard of in the days of lead production, thanks to sophisticated diecasting and injection moulding processes.

Throughout the single-storey factory – where safety signs are multi-lingual with part of its 420-strong labour force drawn from areas of high immigrant populations – the familiar present-day toys of Britains are taking shape from a torrent of components pouring forth from machines like gaudily coloured latticework. A designer sketches away at a drawing board, breastworked by a mound of prototype packaging. A youth supervises a machine that spews out a never-ending stream of plastic grazing sheep. Gun-toting cowboys are being destined for injection-moulding reproduction in a six-mould clamp. A sari-clad girl sits at a bench before a fleet of field-grey scout cars, preparing them for their *Wehrmacht* crews.

A box of pristine green artillery pieces lies awaiting attention in the packing department. The famous Britains' 18-inch howitzers on tractor wheels. 'Take a good look at them,' says Roy Selwyn-Smith. 'They are about the last that will ever go out of here. We are ending their production.' Little boys, it seems, no longer want the 18-inch howitzer, veteran and victor of countless battles with toy soldiers from lead right through into plastic. 'It just isn't selling,' says Smith.

The realization has meant demobilization for one of the last links with Britains' lead soldier heyday. Patented in 1917, 63 years earlier, in its immobile siege version, the 18-incher has been a steady seller through several generations. It was, incidentally, responsible for more damage to potentially valuable soldiers than probably any other single instrument – that is, until the power of its devastating heavy lead shells was emasculated in modern times by the introduction of a 'harmless' flyweight projectile of plastic. Roy Selwyn-Smith agrees: 'Little did we know, when, as kids, we knocked off heads with the howitzer, we were knocking off a fiver, or maybe a tenner, a time.'

The great gun – probably rivalled in popularity only by Britains' old faithful, the 4.7 naval weapon, phased out a little earlier – was being silenced at a time when it was retailing at £5.50, a sum that would have bought you a fair sized army some 60 years previously, as any student of pointless historic-economic comparisons would tell you.

Soon, perhaps, even the modern version of the 18-incher will join the Scots Greys, the Middlesex Regiment, the Gurkhas, the Montenegrins, the Zouaves and the rest in the saleroom catalogues and the collectors' hoards. There are no ghosts of the lead legions in Britains' ultra-modern factory. It is too busy getting on with the business of making headway in a very tough toy world. But on that afternoon, with every department a surge of activity in the run-up to Christmas, the silence of the howitzers was eloquent.

BIBLIOGRAPHY

Allendesalazar, José Manuel, *Coleccionismo de Soldados*, Editorial Everest, Leon, 1978.

Barnes, Major R.M., *Military Uniforms of Britain & the Empire*, and *The Uniforms and history of the Scottish Regiments*, Sphere Books, London, 1972.

Beckett, I.F.W., *Victoria's Wars*, Shire Publications, Aylesbury, Bucks, 1974.

Blum, Peter, *Model Soldiers*, Arms and Armour Press, London, 1971.

Bowling, A.H., *Indian Cavalry Regiments*, Almark Publications, London, 1971.

Britains Ltd *Toy and Model Catalogue*, 1940, reprint by Almark Publications, 1972 (and various other Britains' catalogue from 1910 to 1964).

Caminer, Domenico, *Storia della vita di Federigo II Il Grande*, Presso Francesco Sansoni, Venice, 1787.

Carlyle, Thomas, *History of Frederick the Great*, 1886.

Carman, W.Y., *Model Soldiers*, Charles Lett and Company, London, 1973.

Dilley, Roy, *Scale Model Soldiers*, Almark Publications, London, 1972.

Duffy, Christopher, *The Army Of Frederick the Great*, David & Charles, Newton Abbott, Devon, 1974.

Featherstone, Donald, *Handbook for Model Soldier Collectors*, Kaye & Ward, London, 1969.

Garratt, John G., *Collecting Model Soldiers*, David & Charles, Newton Abbot, Devon, 1975.

— *Model Soldiers A Collector's Guide*, Seeley, Service & Company, London, 1965.

— *Model Soldiers an Illustrated History*, New York Graphic Society, Greenwich, Connecticut, 1972.

Head, Michael G., *Foot Regiments of the Imperial Guard*, and *French Napoleonic Lancer Regiments*, Almark Publications, London, 1973 and 1971.

Johnson, Peter, *Front Line Artists*, Cassell, London, 1978.

Kollbrunner, Curt F., *Figurines d'étain, Soldats de collection*, Office du Livre, Fribourg, Switzerland, 1979.

McKenzie, Ian, *Collecting Old Toy Soldiers*, Batsford, London, 1975.

Milet, Jacques, and Forbes, Robert, *Toy Boats 1870–1955 A Picture History*, Charles Scribner's Sons, New York, 1979.

Mollo, John, *Uniforms of the Seven Years War 1756–63*, Blandford Press, Poole, Dorset, 1977.

O'Brien, Richard, *Collecting Toys*, Books Americana, Florence, Alabama, 1980.

Ortmann, Erwin, *The Collector's Guide to Model Tin Figures*, Studio Vista, London, 1974.

Polaine, Reggie, *The War Toys, No. 1 The Story of Hausser-Elastolin*, New Cavendish Books, London, 1979.

Richards, L.W., *Old British Model Soldiers 1893–1918*, Arms and Armour Press, London, 1970.

Ruddell, Joanne and Ron, *The Britains Collector's Checklist*, Allentown, Pennsylvania, 1980.

Ruddle, John, *Collectors Guide to Britains Model Soldiers*, Model & Allied Publications, 1980.

Seaton, Albert, *Frederick the Great's Army* and *The Austro-Hungarian Army of the Seven Years War*, Osprey, Reading, Berkshire, 1973.

Schroeder, Joseph J., Jr. editor, *The Wonderful World of Toys, Games and Dolls, 1860–1930*, DBI Books, Northfield, Illinois.

Taylor, Arthur, *Discovering Model Soldiers*, Shire Publications, Aylesbury, Bucks, 1972.

Teague, D., *Discovering Modelling for Wargamers*, Shire Publications, Aylesbury, Bucks., 1973.

Théatre de la Guerre présenté en Allemagne, Paris, 1758.

Uniforms of the Seven Years War, Prussia, and Austria, Greenwood & Ball, Thornaby-on-Tees, 1974 and 1975.

Wilkinson-Latham, Robert and Christopher, *Infantry Uniforms*, Blandford Press, London, 1970.

Young, Peter, editor, *The War Game*, Roxby Press, London, 1972.

Articles and pamphlets

Amaya, Mario, 'The *Forbes* Magazine Collection', *Connoisseur*, London, April 1980.

Britain, L.D., *A Brief History of Britains Ltd*, document.

British Toys and Hobbies magazine, 'Dennis Britain Retires', February 1979.

Chelminski, Rudolph, '*Forbes* Museum's little soldiers aren't playthings', *Smithsonian*, August 1980.

Davenport, Elaine, 'The Martial art of Malcolm Forbes', *Now!* magazine, 21 December 1980.

Hopkins, Rosemary Morse, 'The Little Toy Soldier', *Antiques* magazine, USA, 1943.

Howard, Philip, 'Looks at London: Gamages', *The Sunday Times*, 21 March 1972.

Johnson, Peter, 'The Forbes Collection', *Military Modelling*, UK, November 1979.

— 'Holiday in Tangier', *Old Toy Soldier Newsletter*, December 1979, and February 1980.

— 'How to recruit your own private army', *House and Garden*, October 1976.

— 'Old Britains', *International Toy and Doll Collector*, 1979.

— 'Old Soldiers', *Art and Antiques Weekly*, London, 20 December 1975.

— 'A peaceful and agreeable way to go to war', *House and Garden*, January 1980.

— 'A private army in Tangier', *International Toy and Doll Collector*, January 1980.

Jones, J. Edward, *Looking for a good hobby?*, published by Moulded Miniatures, Chicago, 1948.

Kurts, Henry I., 'Toy Soldiers Never Die, They just Turn to Profit', *American Way*, December 1979.

Leitch, David, 'How to live like an old-fashioned millionaire', *The Sunday Times Magazine*, 31 August 1980.

Perry, Phillip M., 'Soldiers parade on living-room shelves', *Christian Science Monitor*, 21 March 1978.

Schumach, Murray, 'It's a small world', *Antiques World*, USA, 1979.

Stars, Judith, 'Trooping of the Colour in Wales', *The Guardian*, London, 22 June 1927.

Swann, R., *There's something about a soldier – a short Britains history*, written for Britains, circa 1978.

The Toy and Fancy Goods Trader, From War to Peace, March 1923.

Wade, Shamus O.D., *Nostalgia Models The 'New Old' Toy Soldiers*, leaflet and history.

In addition many articles on various toy and model soldier subjects in *Old Toy Soldier Newsletter*, USA, and *The Bulletin of the British Model Soldier Society*.

INDEX